The Bengali Book
of
English Verse

The Bengali Book of English Verse

THEODORE DOUGLAS DUNN

GYAN

Published by

Gyan Publishing House
5, Ansari Road
Daryaganj, New Delhi-110002
Phone: 011-47034999, 9811692060
E-mail: books@gyanbooks.com

Distribution Network
gyanbooks.com
India, USA, Canada, UK, Australia

ISBN: 978-93-7133-193-7 (PB)

First Published, 1918

2nd Impression 2025

Printed at: Gyan Press, Delhi.

THE BENGALI BOOK OF ENGLISH VERSE
Author: THEODORE DOUGLAS DUNN

The Bengali Book of English Verse

selected and arranged

by

THEODORE DOUGLAS DUNN

with a foreword

by

SIR RABINDRANATH TAGORE.

LONGMANS, GREEN, AND CO.
HORNBY ROAD, BOMBAY
6 OLD COURT HOUSE STREET, CALCUTTA
167 MOUNT ROAD, MADRAS
LONDON AND NEW YORK
1918

TO

HIS EXCELLENCY

THE EARL OF RONALDSHAY

THIS MEMORIAL OF BENGALI ACHIEVEMENT

IN

THE LANGUAGE OF THE BRITISH EMPIRE.

Contents.

Acknowledgments.

Many of the poems of this book have been taken from magazines no longer in circulation, and from volumes long out of print. In the examination of these sources I have been greatly helped by Mr. S. C. Sanial, Secretary of the Calcutta Historical Society. Mr. J. A. Chapman of the Imperial Library has given much assistance in procuring forgotten but interesting material.

Of living authors who have allowed their verse to appear in this collection, my thanks are due to Mrs. Sarojini Naidu, to Mr. P. R. Das and to Professor Manmohan Ghose. With the exception of one extract, reproduced with the permission of Messrs. Elkin Mathews from "Love Songs and Elegies," the poems of Professor Ghose included in this book are published for the first time. For such as have appeared in the "Presidency College Magazine" I am indebted to the managers of that journal.

In many cases the copyright of books now out of print rests with the family of the author. Here I have to make many grateful acknowledgments. Mr. J. C. Dutt who introduced me to the "Dutt Family Album," published in 1870 by Messrs. Longmans Green, has allowed the reproduction of the verse of his father, Omesh Chunder Dutt. Mrs. G. C. Dutt, Professor B. C. Dutt and Mr. S. C. Dutt have given me permission to include the poems of their relatives. For the work of Sir Jotindra Mohan Tagore I am indebted to his son, the present Maharaja. The members of the Ramkrishna Mission have given one of the poems of the Swami Vivekananda. Mr. R. K. Ghose and Mr. D. C. Mullick have allowed me to select from the writings of the late Nobo

Kissen Ghose (Ram Sharma). Mr. M. Dutta and the Committee of the Barnagore Victoria School have permitted the inclusion of poems by Roby Dutt.

In the spelling of Bengali names I have adhered in every case to the forms adopted by the authors themselves; and these, in some cases, peculiar forms have been confirmed by the relatives of the writers now deceased.

Messrs. Heinemann have allowed me to select from the poems of Mrs. Sarojini Naidu; and Messrs. Kegan Paul have granted the use of three poems by Toru Dutt and of one poem by Romesh Chander Dutt. The latter's translations from the Mahabharata have been given by Messrs. Dent. Mr. J. N. Bose, the author and publisher of the Bengali biography of Michael Dutt, has given two of the latter's sonnets from that work. Mr. W. I. Keir has generously furnished the cover design.

No anthology of this kind could appear with assurance, were it not introduced by the author of the Gitanjali. I have to acknowledge with thankful appreciation the foreword of Sir Rabindranath Tagore who has allowed me to retain the translation of his poem on Sir Jagadis Chandra Bose.

Foreword.

The following anthology has its greatest interest in being a self-recording evidence of the earliest response that Bengal gave to the touch of the West. I think we can safely assert that she is the only country in the Orient which has shown any distinct indication of being thrilled by the voice of Europe as it came to her through literature. We are not concerned with a critical estimate of Bengal's earliest literary adventures in the perilous fields of a foreign tongue. But the important fact is this, that while there are other eastern countries captivated by the sight of the immense power and prosperity which Europe presented to us, Bengal has been stirred by the force of new ideas breaking upon her from the western horizon. One of its earliest effects upon our students was to rouse them into an aggressive antagonism against all orthodox conventions, irrespective of their merits. It was a sudden self-assertion of life after its repression for ages. This shock, which roused Bengal, mainly came through literature, and a great part of her energy followed the same channel of literature for its expression.

The most memorable instance of the working of ideas in Bengal in the time of her early contact of mind with Europe, has been Rammohan Roy's message of life to India,—a life centering in the spiritual idea of the all-pervading oneness of God, as inculcated in the Upanishads, and comprehending in its circumference all varieties of human activities from the moral down to the political. It was a call to move and fully to live, not from a blind love of movement, but as directed by an inner guidance coming from the heart of India's own wisdom.

Though the above instance does not directly touch the literary side of our life, yet I cite it to show that it was through her sensitiveness to ideas that Bengal has been deeply moved from the time of her first acquaintance with Europe. And ever since, the same formation of ideals has been going on through various stages of action and reaction. Those who have the talent and love for constructive work can show their productions in a palpable form and with a rapidity of results. But Idea works in the depth of life, bringing about fundamental changes in the very soil and seeds, and sprouts forth from the unseen in its own time in a living creative form. Its early energies are engaged and seem wasted in work of destruction, in explosions of discontent, in constant vacillation in choice, thus easily lending itself to the charge of volatility and indecision. But life has its side which is vigorously destructive and full of uncertainties and contradictions. The signs of perturbation so evident in Bengal, in her social and religious life, in her intellectual adjustments, only show that creative ideas are at work in the centre of her being. I trust I do not merely prove my patriotic bias by saying that, of all countries in the East, Bengal is most earnestly engaged in the exploration of life's ideal. All the great personalities she has produced in the modern time have presented to us according to their light, some ideal solution of life's inner problem. We are fully aware that this is not all that humanity requires, that there are other questions more immediately importunate which have to be answered if we must live; and there are signs that we are beginning actively to recognise this important fact. But all the same we must confess, that whatever it may have cost us, we have dealt more with the ideas that move our soul by kindling our imagination than with acquiring and arranging materials to help us in our struggle for existence. This has led to an active conflict in Bengal between the Old and the New, a constant shifting of her outlooks upon life and an unrest owing to her groping for something positive, by which she can win for good her own true place in the world.

Our present age of renaissance began its career with an exaggerated faith in the foreign and the external, to find out at last that life is a process of constant self-unfolding, whose impulse comes from the centre of its own being. In Bengal we meet with all the different stages of this development, and therefore, more than in other parts of India, it is here that love of imitation of the West runs to excess, pompously proud of its tawdriness and incongruity. On the other hand in Bengal have been originated all the recent movements for the seeking of truth that is our national heritage. The West, which at first drew us on to itself, has forcibly flung us back upon an intense consciousness of our personality. The breath of inspiration, coming from the West, has kindled the original spark in us into a flame that lay smothered in the ashes of dead habits and rigidity of traditional forms. This has been illustrated by the course our literature has taken, almost completely abandoning its earlier foreign bed, finding its natural channel in the mother tongue. The following collection of English poems written by Bengali authors also proves it, in which the earlier writings are timorously imitative, while the later ones boldly burn with their own fire, daring to challenge time's judgment with their claim of immortality. I believe foreign readers, while reading this book, will find much to think of in the fact that Bengal's response through literature to the call of the West is something unique in the history of the modern East. It has a future, for it is quickened with life, and it carries within itself a hope that one day it will become a great channel for communication of ideas between the adventurous West and the East of the immemorial tranquillity.

RABINDRANATH TAGORE.

Introduction.

The verse collected in this volume represents about one hundred years of poetical effort; and has its origin in England's introduction into India of western education. It is worth recording that the first volume of Bengali verse in English appeared five years before Thomas Babington Macaulay gave judgment in favour of the teaching of English in Indian schools and colleges. The fact is significant. It shows that the movement towards English instruction had begun before the administration of Lord William Bentinck, and had achieved definite results before the famous Resolution of 1835.

Early English Teachers in Bengal.

From this date the character of education in India was fixed. An educational policy had been conceived and adopted—briefly, the teaching of English language and literature. It was the good fortune of Bengal that this policy was born in the spacious days when the literary life of England was brilliant and vigorous; and when, amongst the English in India, there were men who had lived largely in the life of their time. The shadow of a few great names lies broad over the scholastic history of the early 19th century in Bengal. Sir William Jones had handed down a rich scholarly tradition. Dr. John Leyden, the friend and colleague of Sir Walter Scott, had kept alive the fires of Border Song amid the fevers of Bengal and Java. Bishop Heber was a poet of rare delicacy as well as a strenuous traveller and priest. Before he left India in 1832, Horace Hayman Wilson had laid deep the foundations of his Sanskrit learning; and Henry Meredith Parker, by his witty occasional poems and the versatility of his talent, had delighted the English and Indian community up to the date of his departure in 1842. One of the earliest teachers of the Hindu College was himself a poet deeply imbued with the Byronic spirit. Henry Derozio was trained in the Dhurrumtollah Academy of John Drummond, a Scottish dominie of the old type ; and, while engaged as an Indigo planter, he began to contribute verse to the Calcutta journals. In 1818 he was appointed to the Hindu College as a teacher of English literature and history ; but the orthodox took fright at his outspoken treatment of sacred themes, and he had to resign his post. In 1831 after the enjoyment of much poetical effort and a few stimulating friendships, he died of cholera. His fluent and impassioned poetry brought him recognition in India, and contributed to his undoubted influence over his students who regarded him as a teacher of genius. In the Hindu College he established the tradition of an enthusiastic study of English literature which, on sounder and more scholarly lines, was carried on by David Lester Richardson.

To this teacher modern Bengal owes much. Like many Englishmen whose names are still alive in the East, he came to India as a soldier in the army of the Company. On his return to England in search of health, he engaged in literary work in London, published his poems and started a paper called The Weekly Review. The collapse of this journal in 1827 compelled Richardson's return to Bengal. In 1835 he acted as aide-de-camp to Lord William Bentinck ; and in the following year, through the influence of Macaulay, he was appointed professor and, later, principal of the Hindu College. From this date, until his retirement in 1861, his career was definitely that of a teacher and man of letters. In addition to his miscellaneous literary work, Richardson was responsible for two publications of great value and interest. The first was the Bengal Annual, a collection of prose and verse that appeared on seven occasions between the years 1830 and 1836. To this work Indian and English authors contributed ; and its pages make a delightful thesaurus of the outstanding names of the period. The second was the voluminous Selections from the British Poets. This compilation was undertaken at the suggestion of Macaulay and produced in 1840. Its chief interest lies in the anthology of British-Indian poetry—the first and best anthology of its kind—which the author compiled and added as an appendix to the major work.

The Hindu College.

It is pleasant to attempt to reconstruct the life of the Hindu College in these early years. Its teachers were men of established literary reputation ; and its patrons have written their names large upon the history of their age. There are frequent contemporary references to the quaint figure of David Hare, with long blue coat adorned by large brass buttons, moving through the class rooms, or attending the debates of the academic association. No less a personage than Thomas Babington Macaulay, who admitted that one of his compensations for exile in Calcutta was to hear Richardson read Shakespeare, has put on record his work done as an examiner for the Committee of Public Instruction. In the present age of conflicting pedagogic theories this makes curious reading. He speaks of examining on the texts of Shakespeare, Bacon, Cowley and Swift ; and writes with characteristic absence of humour or hesitation—"I gave a subject for an essay, the comparative advantage of the study of poetry and the study of history." Whatever the Bengali students made of this majestic theme, there can be no doubt that, with Richardson for teacher and Macaulay for examiner, the atmosphere of their work was saturated with the literary

2

spirit, and their labours were not confined to any petty scholastic routine. The day of the Indian Universities was not yet. The rush of modern competition transforming school and college courses into an immediate means towards desperately desired ends, had not set in. There was no examination fetish, nor any extensive system of cheap secondary education. German philology had not as yet invaded the fair domain of letters. The aim of college work was to learn the English language; and towards this end the good fortune of Bengal provided patrons and teachers who combined scholarship with culture, and who had lived largely in the life of their time.

The First Bengali Writers of English Verse.

To the encouragement and example of these men may be traced whatever English verse was produced by Bengali writers in the first half of the 19th century. This was not large in quantity, and was the work of three authors: Kasiprasad Ghose, whose Minstrel appeared in 1830; Rajnarain Dutt who dedicated to Richardson his Osmyn, an Arabian tale, in 1841; and Michael Madhusudan Dutt whose Captive Ladie, published in 1849, is the most ambitious poetical effort of any Bengali writer. Michael Dutt is a curiously interesting figure. He was educated in the Hindu College, and won the friendship and patronage of Richardson who encouraged his bent towards poetry. In 1843 he became a Christian; and after residence in the Bishop's College, he went to Madras. Here, in 1849, he produced The Captive Ladie; and thereafter devoted himself to the study and cultivation of Bengali literature. In 1861 his classical narrative poem, Meghanadbadh, and his translation of the notorious Nil Darpan, brought him prominently into notice. In the following year he went to England and studied law; but his subsequent career was not fortunate;

and in 1873 he died in poverty. His name is beloved by his countrymen ; and Ram Sharma's memorial lines, quoted in this volume, have found a ready response in Bengal.

The Dutt Family Album.

The success of Michael Dutt stimulated the brilliant band of relatives who produced in London, in 1870, The Dutt Family Album. This book must be of abiding interest and value to the student of literary history in India. Published by the house of Longmans, it is an anthology compiled from the original poems of Govin, Omesh, Greece and Hur Chunder Dutt. In the preface the authors claim consideration for their compilation as a curiosity, and as the work of foreigners educated out of England. Up to this date no Bengali writer had been trained in Europe. While it is true that Michael Dutt studied law in London, his production of the Captive Ladie belongs to the year 1849, before he had left Madras. The Dutt Family Album, therefore, may be taken to represent the older school of Bengali poetry in English. It was the compilation of men whose encouragement to literary work was received from such enthusiastic teachers as Richardson, and whose academic career began and ended in the Hindu College of Calcutta. The literary merits of this book, carefully judged in the light of the special circumstances of its production, are considerable. The quality of the verse, the range and variety of theme, the command of various metrical forms, and the restraint and dignity of the style, are everywhere pleasing. The most notable of the four authors were Govin and Omesh, who contributed 66 and 73 pieces out of the total of 197. Indian history, legend and landscape, the picturesque elements of the Christian and the Hindu faith, and such ideas as would attract an oriental in his first intercourse with the west, provide the themes of their verse.

Hur Chunder Dutt began to write early. In 1851 he produced in Calcutta a small volume of poems called Fugitive Pieces. Much of this was reprinted twenty years later in his second volume named Lotus Leaves. Both works are slight; but they contain a pleasing variety of themes drawn from Indian history, and the verse is everywhere graceful. His part in the Album amounted to eleven poems in all. Greece contributed forty-seven separate pieces; and in 1887 published with Messrs. Fisher Unwin a separate volume of poems entitled Cherry Blossoms. In this work several of the earlier contributions to the Album were reprinted, but the greater number of the poems were new. The book was carefully produced and contains much of interest and value. The author had specialised in the difficult sonnet form; and of the 165 poems of the book, no less than 70 are sonnets. The subjects of these poems are as varied as the author's experiences derived from much travel in Europe and India. With this last volume of Greece Chunder Dutt the poetical effort of these gifted relatives may be said to have reached its close. Their achievement was creditable both in its quality and in its consistency. That portion of their work embodied in the Dutt Family Album will remain as a memorial of a gifted family, and as a testimony to the influence of those English teachers who were the first to encourage the higher learning in the city of Calcutta.

Later Poets.

The successful treatment of Indian historical themes, of which there are frequent illustrations in the Album, was continued by Shoshee Chunder Dutt who published in 1878 his Vision of Sumeru and other Poems, a compilation of verse written at any time in the preceding twenty years. The greater part of this volume is taken up with historical and legendary poems of such interest as to cause regret that their author did not seek inspiration more assiduously in the romantic history of India. To the year 1881 belongs the work of the Maharajah Sir Jotindra Mohan Tagore whose Flights of Fancy may still be read with pleasure. This is a slight volume of occasional verse dealing with a variety of pleasing topics, and exhibiting a cultivated command of English metre. Of the writers of this time the most voluminous was Nobo Kissen Ghose who wrote under the pseudonym of Ram Sharma. His verse is scattered throughout a number of magazines that appeared in Calcutta between the years 1878 and 1901. In 1886 he published his blank verse poem, The Last Day, in which are embodied interesting portraits of such outstanding men as David Hare, Rammohan Roy, Lord Canning, and Dr. Duff. His occasional poems are distinguished by the vigour of their expression and the independence of their author's mind. He dealt frequently with social and political themes; and his outspokenness was greatly emphasised by the refinement and energy of his language. Ram Sharma was born in the year of Queen Victoria's accession, and died in 1918. His long career is a link with the past. While he was educated in the Oriental Seminary under Captain Francis Palmer, and may have missed the influence of Richardson and the Hindu College, he belongs to the period that includes the work of the ten poets already named.

The Value of this Poetical Work.

It may well be asked what is the value of the poetry produced by these writers. That they were devoted disciples of the art of letters is clear enough; but more than disciples they were not. To the student of Indian educational history their work must be of abiding interest; but in the larger world of literature, it can hold no distinctive place. Such poetry as they produced was Indian only in so far as it was written in Bengal, and was the result of education received therein; and it is scarcely an exaggeration to say that here its oriental character begins and ends. Even the excellence of Michael Dutt lies chiefly in his ability to follow his metrical masters; while most of his successors approach the history of their country as if they had no part in its heritage. In dealing with the intimacies of the Hindu faith, it might be expected that these writers would produce something of unique interest. There are frequent odes on Indian deities and on religious festivals, but none of them are really arresting in their sincerity, or provide anything that is essentially eastern in conception. When Kasiprasad Ghose addresses Saraswati in this manner—

> Goddess of every mental grace,
> And virtue of the soul,
> Which high exalt the human race,
> And lead to glory's goal,
>
> 'Tis thou who bid'st the infant mind,
> Its growing thoughts display,
> Which lay within it undefined
> In regular array.

—he is merely re-echoing the jingle of such 18th century rhymesters as William Hayley, and fails utterly to reproduce the atmosphere of his own faith. It is reasonable to expect from an eastern poet something that a western cannot give. But the reader of this literature will look in vain for anything that is peculiarly and exclusively oriental. Emerson, in one of his briefest occasional poems, obsessed by the conception of Brahma, has conjured up a whole world of eastern religious mysticism—

> If the red slayer think he slays,
> Or if the slain think he is slain,
> They know not well the subtle ways
> I keep and pass and turn again.

Far or forgot to me is near ;
Shadow and sunlight are the same ;
The vanquished gods to me appear ;
And one to me are shame and fame.

They reckon ill who leave me out ;
When me they fly, I am the wings ;
I am the doubter and the doubt,
And I the hymn the Brahmin sings.

Sir Alfred Lyall in his poem, Siva, has looked through and beyond the sensuous imagery of the Hindu temple to the conception of those terrible powers that hold man and rule his destiny. In his verse the majesty and terror of an ancient faith are made to appeal from their own oriental setting. Sir Edwin Arnold, in such a brief lyric as The Song of the Serpent Charmers, has created the true atmosphere of the east. But the Bengali writers now under consideration appear to be at work in some strangely neutral zone of the imagination, and to be uninfluenced by the colour and atmosphere of their environment. The reason may be that these early writers in an alien tongue were anxious to anglicise not only their vocabulary but their ideas. If so, to contrast their efforts with the achievements of the three western poets already named, would be unfair. The latter deliberately sought the eastern point of view and the eastern atmosphere ; while the former were content to exhibit their skill in the handling of a newly acquired and difficult language. They were amongst the earliest students of English in India ; and while they have failed to contribute anything of real value to the literature of the Empire, they have at least justified their own publications as illustrating the successful study of a great literature and a difficult speech. They have laid the foundation of the work of several poets still in our midst ; and have provided the curious student of

Anglo-Bengali verse with the pleasure to be found in the perusal of all clever literary exercise.

The Modern School.

The tradition established by these writers was broken by the daughter of Govin Chunder Dutt. This lady may be justly described as the founder of the modern school of English poetry in Bengal. In two ways she differs from her predecessors—in her European education received in England and France; and in her acceptance of oriental themes at the very time when, by her talented application, she had forged for herself an instrument of expression from two difficult European languages. Toru Dutt was born in 1856; and, at the age of 13, was taken to Europe by her parents. In 1872, after various courses of study in London and Paris, she returned to Calcutta. Four years later she died of consumption. Into her tragically brief career, there was crowded a literary accomplishment little short of marvellous. She was an enthusiastic student of French, and wrote that language with ease and precision. Her romance, Le Journal de Mlle. D'Arvers, was published in 1879, three years after the appearance of her first work, A Sheaf Gleaned in French Fields. The history of the latter book is curious. Mr. Edmund Gosse tells how, in the office of the *Examiner*, he was lamenting with the editor, the famous William Minto, the dearth of new books of merit. As he was speaking, the postman brought in a packet from India which contained a curiously coloured pamphlet printed at the Saptahik Sambad Press of Bhowanipore. Those acquainted with the binding and type of the Calcutta presses will understand the amused surprise of the London editor when he handled an orange-tinted cover and read the mysterious names on the title page. Minto handed the book to Mr. Gosse who, glancing at it later, happened to light upon this rendering of Victor Hugo's serenade :—

Still barred thy doors! The far east glows,
The morning wind blows fresh and free,
Should not the hour that wakes the rose
Awaken also thee?

All look for thee, Love, Light and Song;
Light, in the sky deep red above,
Song, in the lark of pinion strong,
And in my heart, true love.

There was sufficient beauty and skill in these lines to arrest the attention of any critic; and in 1881 Mr. Gosse wrote the preface to the first collection of Toru Dutt's original poems entitled Ancient Ballads and Legends of Hindustan. This volume, published by Messrs. Kegan Paul, contains her latest and best work. Unlike her predecessors, Toru Dutt did not wilfully anglicise her ideas. For the first time in literature of this kind, there is struck a genuinely Indian note that reveals the sincerity of a mind proud of the intellectual traditions of its native land. The technical skill of this poetess is superior to that of any of her predecessors; and this, in view of her extreme youth, is little short of amazing. Her verse is finely knit, vigorous and of a pleasing variety. It is never obviously imitative, and moves with such freedom and independence as are inseparable from genuinely creative work. Toru Dutt was nurtured in a literary family; but this environment does not wholly explain the achievement of this gifted lady whose genius was so tragically denied maturity. She brought to her work a certain fervid originality that, before the end of the 19th century, redeemed Bengali literature in English from the commonplace. She is the first of the new school of Indian poets, and both in England and India her place and her memory are assured.

Poets in our midst.

Of living authors whose work has been illustrated in this volume, it is unnecessary to speak at length. There is much in the life of modern India to foster intellectual and artistic activity. A perfervid political enthusiasm; the intense realisation of racial and national sentiment; a fuller knowledge of India's intellectual heritage, and a careful balancing of the rival claims of eastern and western culture—these may well stir the artistic impulse of a people naturally endowed with the gift of expression. But only two writers of English verse have come to prominence; and one of them is not specially concerned with eastern thought or life.

Manmohan Ghose left Oxford in 1892, having won distinction in the classical schools. In 1898 he published with Messrs. Elkin Mathews a small volume of poems entitled Love Songs and Elegies; and if he were to produce nothing more, his position as a true poet and as an exquisite artist would demand recognition. Unfortunately the whole work of this gifted author is not yet accessible in any single volume. Much of it has appeared in magazine literature; and of this, one poem—A Song of Britannia—is the finest poetic expression of patriotism yet called forth by the war. Manmohan Ghose has brought to the work of a poet a fine scholarship and a cultivated critical taste. In his poetry there is a subtler melody and a more convincing exhibition of technical skill than have yet appeared in the history of Bengali verse in English.

His contemporary, the poetess Sarojini Naidu, shares his fastidious choice of language, but seeks a more popular fluency of rhythm. This lady, like her gifted predecessor, Toru Dutt, was educated in London, and has already found an eager audience in England and India. Her popularity may be in part explained by her skilful treatment of eastern themes, and by her representation of these in a genuinely oriental light. It is significant that the task of wedding the rich vocabulary of England's poetry to purely oriental subjects has been accomplished by two Indian women. The feminine imagination will not endure expatriation, and clings tenaciously to the subtle memory of its origins. After half a century of barren literary exercise, Toru Dutt was the first to find in her own land an inspiration for her genius ; and her achievement is being triumphantly repeated in the work of her accomplished successor.

The story of Bengali adventure in the realm of English poetry is not yet complete. But it is a pleasing task to put on record a century of this endeavour, and to trace its progress towards a rich fulfilment.

T. O. D. DUNN.

United Service Club,
Calcutta, December 1918.

KASIPRASAD GHOSE,

1809–1873.

Dasahara.

Glorious river! thee of yore
Siva on his tresses bore,
When thou didst thy rapid flow
Take unto this world below,
From the peak of Himalay,
Where thy lucid waters stray,
Dispensing to the gods above
Purity and holy love.

Propitious river! by thy grace
Royal Sagar's numerous race,
Though burned to ashes by the fire
Of the saintly sage's ire,
Enjoyed the bright, unchanging hours,
Smiling round the emerald bowers,
And bringing in the heavenly sphere
Joys which only circle there.

Holy stream! thou dost bestow
Freedom from each earthly woe,
Destroying all the sins that be
Pertaining to humanity,
And ensure at being's close,
Sweet and undisturbed repose.
Nay! even the deities love to lave
Their forms of glory in thy wave.

Beauteous river! on thy spray
The lotos famed in ancient lay—

Whose chaplets and whose odours sweet,
Goddess ! to thee are offerings meet—
In gladness doth its leaves unfold
Full to the morning's beam of gold,
As if inspired with the love
Of the majestic sun above.

Dreadful river ! in thy waves
His length the alligator laves,
And sharks and sea-hogs round him play,
Glad with the hope of human prey.
When summer with the hot sun crowned,
Showers her dazzling splendour round,
And brings forth in our Indian bowers
Refulgent days and lovely flowers.

To a Young Hindu Widow.

Ah, fair one ! lone as desert flower,
  Whose bloom and beauty are in vain ;
How dark was that too fatal hour,
  Which brought thee lasting grief and pain !

What is the world to thee forlorn !
  Thine every path is desolate,
From all enjoyments rudely torn,
  How drear and comfortless thy fate !

What pity, friendless, helpless, poor !
  That such should be thine early lot—
Doomed to remain for ever more
  As if thou in this world wert not.

And is there none—O ! can it be ?
  None warm or friendly in thy cause ?
Has pitiless humanity
  Forgot its sacred ties and laws ?

The rigours of a life austere,
Followed by every fear and shame,
Await thee as thy portion here :
What is thy being but a name ?

Thou may'st not, dar'st not, must not hope
A joy upon the world beneath ;
But thou must e'er with sorrows cope,
Sorrows which only end in death.

And thou art doomed to be at strife
For ever with thyself, to quell
The very elements of life,
And every brighter thought repel.

Is this the all, or should it be
The all that here to thee is left ?
And must the world remain to thee
A scene of every charm bereft ?

Storm and Rain.

The mighty demons of the storm have met
In battle fierce. Relentless anger fires
Their bosoms, proud of desolating power.
Their swords in rapid wavings flash ; and oft
In lightning gleams illume the darkened earth.
Hark ! how they vaunt in thunder deep and loud,
And madly howling, rave athwart the arch
Of heaven ; convolving Gunga's waters deep ;
Which wildly running to and fro, dismayed,
Or upward bounding high, appear as if
They wish to break loose from their beds to fly
The tempest's rage. Beneath its headlong speed

Reft of her beauties green, fair Nature quakes
Affrighted ; and upon the plain are strewed
Leaves, arms, and trunks of many a giant tree
Felled by their wrath.

But soon unto the clouds,
Which darkly frown upon the earth, as though
In hate and envy, fly the tempest fiends ;
And there, bound by some unknown, powerful charm,
They roar as if once more they would descend
And sweep the world before their furious course
Blasting the fairest scenes of Nature fair
With demon strength and hate.

The ruthless storm
Is past. Cloud upon cloud is piled along
The darksome brow of yonder skies, enshrouding
The face of the bright Sun, who o'er the earth
High on his throne of ether, erst did reign
In splendour cloudless, dazzling, yet serene.
The gathering darkness deepens round ; as if
The spell of awe hath bound the face of heaven—
The spell which but the poet's gifted eye
Can trace ; and but his flexile heart can feel
Attracted.

Now the floods of heaven unsealed
At once burst forth in torrents, deluging
The shrinking earth : and as the clouds become
Dispersed and thinner by the wandering breeze,
The glories of the broad, meridian Sun
Descend and sparkle. But the firmament
Still pours its genial springs of crystal rain,
Which, brightened by the solar beams, appear
Like showers of liquid radiance falling down,
A blessed gift to Man from favouring heaven.
The little shrubs, which ere long drooped beneath

The summer Sun's refulgent noontide, now
Reviving, raise their heads and put forth all
Their verdurous majesty. Each leaf is decked
With drops of rain, like pearls and diamonds bright
Quivering in the gentle gale, which breathes
Delightful fragrance round.

To a Dead Crow.

Gay minstrel of the Indian clime!
How oft at morning's rosy prime
When thou didst sing in *caw*, *caw* numbers,
Vexed I've awoke from my sweet slumbers,
And to avoid that hateful sound,
That plagues a head howe'er profound,
Have walked out in my garden, where
Beside the tank, in many a square,
Sweet lilies, jasmines, roses bloom,
Far from those trees within whose gloom
Of foliage thick, thou hadst thy nest
From daily toil at night to rest.

Now lifeless on the earth, cold, bare,
Devoid alike of joy and care,
The offals of my meal no more
Attract thee as they did before.
There's rubbish scattered round thee, but
Thy heart is still, thine eyes are shut.
No more that blunt yet useful beak
From carcases thy food can seek,
Or catch the young unheeded mouse,
Which from the flooring of my house
Urged by its hapless luck, would stray
And bask beneath the solar ray.

Gay minstrel ! ne'er had Death before
Its dart destructive, sharpened more
To pierce a gayer, mortal heart
Than thine, which ah ! hath felt the smart !
Though life no more is warm in thee,
Yet thou dost look as though 't may be
That life in thee is full and warm ;
Not cruel death could mar thy form ;
Thy features, one and all, possess
Still, still their former ugliness.
They are in truth the very same
The Indian Crow hath, known to fame.

Oh ! may when death hath closed these eyes,
And freed from earthly bondage, flies
The spirit to eternity,
Stretched at full length I lie like thee,
On mother earth's cold lap, so ne'er
To spin such verses out I'll dare,
And please the public ear again
With such discordant, silly strain,
As thou didst once delight to pour
At morn or noon, or evening hour.
In sooth I promise this shall be
My last line in addressing thee.

RAJNARAIN DUTT,

1824–1889.

Song.

The Beduins have mounted their steeds, and afar
Their Cohorts advance in the proud ranks of war,
They have braced on the shield, and the sword by their side
And forth are they gone on a foray to ride.

On, on through the forest they gallop away,
Like the prowler that rushes in wrath on the prey ;
At the clang of their steeds, and the clash of their arm,
The owl and the tiger will start in alarm.

O'er hill, and o'er valley they ride with the blast,
Ah ! blood shall soon mark where those footsteps have past,
Like the lightning they come, like the lightning they go,
To work out destruction and slaughter and woe.

For the right of their chieftain the broad-sword they draw,
Revenge is their leader, and vengeance their law ;
And reckless alike of disgrace or renown,
Their highest ambition's to crush the foe down.

Ah, soon will those hills with the thunder be riven,
And soon will the proud steed to battle be driven,
The smoke of the village, and shrieks of the prey,
Shall yield to stern war the red spoil of decay.

MICHAEL MADHUSUDAN DUTT,

1824–1873.

The Captive Ladie.

The Captive Ladie is the most considerable verse production in English from the pen of a Bengali writer. For this reason alone it deserves more lengthy representation than other works. Concerning its theme the author himself writes :—

"The following tale is founded on a circumstance pretty generally known in India, and, if I mistake not, noticed by some European writers. A little before the famous Indian expedition of Mahmud of Ghuzni, the King of Kanauj celebrated the "Raj-shooio Jugum" or, as I have translated it in the text, the "Feast of Victory." Almost all the contemporary Princes, being unable to resist his power, attended it, with the exception of the King of Delhi, who, being a lineal descendant of the great Pandu Princes—the heroes of the far-famed Mahabharat of Vyasa—refused to sanction by his presence the assumption of a dignity—for the celebration of this Festival was an universal assertion of claims to being considered as the lord paramount over the whole country—which by right of descent belonged to his family alone. The King of Kanauj highly incensed at this refusal, had an image of gold made to represent the absent chief. On the last day of the Feast, the King of Delhi, having, with a few chosen followers, entered the palace in disguise, carried off this image, together, as some say, with one of the Princesses Royal whose hand he had once solicited but in vain, owing to his obstinate maintenance of the rights of his ancient house. The fair Princess, however, was retaken and sent to a solitary castle to be out of the way of her pugnacious lover, who eventually effected her escape in the disguise of a Bhat or Indian Troubadour. The King of

Kanauj never forgave this insult, and, when Mahmud invaded the kingdom of Delhi, sternly refused to aíd his son-in-law in expelling a foe, who soon after crushed him also. I have slightly deviated from the above story in representing my heroine as sent to confinement before the celebration of the "Feast of Victory."

CANTO FIRST.

The star of Eve is in the sky,
But pale it shines and tremblingly,
As if the solitude around,
So vast, so wild, without a bound,
Hath in its softly throbbing breast
Awak'd some maiden fear—unrest:

* * * *

'Tis eve—the dew's on leaf and flower,
The soft breeze in the moon-lit bower,
And fire-flies with pale gleaming gems
Upon their fairy diadems,
Like winged stars now walk the deep
Of space soft-hushed in dewy sleep,
And people every leaf and tree
With beauty and with radiancy.

There's light upon the heaving stream,
And music sweet as heard in dream,
And many a star upon its breast
Is calmly pillow'd unto rest,
While there, as on a silver throne,
All melancholy, veil'd, alone,
Beneath the pale Moon's colder ray,
The Bride of him—the Lord of Day,
In silence droops, as in lone bower
The love-lorn maid at twilight hour.

She looks not on the smiling sky,
The wide expanse blue, far and high,
She looks not on the stars above
Throbbing like bosoms breathing love ;
Nor lists she to the breeze so gay,
Which whispers round in wanton play,
And stirs soft waves of starry gleam
To wake her from that moody dream.

The moon-light's on yon frowning pile,
But oh ! how faint and pale its smile !
Methinks yon high and gloomy tow'r
And battlement and faded bow'r,
With awful hush and solitude
Have chill'd its soft and joyous mood.

This fortress is the prison of the captive princess whose guards deplore the duty that keeps them from the more active service of their time :—

"You tell me that yon captive lone
Would grace the proudest monarch's throne,
And that from regal bowers she came,
And halls whose splendour has no name,
Because she lov'd some chief whose pride
Would stoop not, e'en to win his bride,
To her proud father ; for his hand
Could wield as well the warrior brand,
And his the race who ne'er hath shown
Submission to a stranger's throne ;
And ne'er hath lowly bent the knee
To Powers of this wide earth that be !
I grieve to hear her piteous tale ;
And must such cruel fate bewail ;
I grieve to hear that maiden fair
Should shed the tear of dark Despair,

And dim the lustre of her eye,
And blanche her cheek's soft, rosy dye.
But why should warrior come to dwell
Like captive in his lightless cell,
Nor list to charger's neigh so shrill
Re-echoed far from hill to hill,
Nor midst the battle's maddening roar,
Nor on wide plains all bath'd in gore,
Wield his bright blade where foe-men throng
To spare the weak—to crush the strong!

" They say the Crescent's on the gales
Which whisper in our moon-lit vales:
They say that Moslem feet have trod
The fanes of him—the Bramin's God;
And that from western realms afar
Fast flows the tide of furious war,
Like torrent from the mountain glen,
Like lion from his bloody den,
Like eagle from the aery peak
Of skiey mount and high and bleak.
What—must we here on this lone isle
Watch yon pale Goddess' pensive smile,
Like cravens who will shrink to bleed
E'en for the Hero's deathless meed!"

The guards decide to while the weary hours with song; and one of their number, a soldier-minstrel or troubadour, tells the story of the Feast of Victory:—

" The Raja sat in his gorgeous hall
In pomp the proudest earth had known,
While monarchs bow'd them to his thrall,
And knelt them lowly round his throne,
The brightest gems of the South lay there
And the North's treasures from afar,

And of the East and West so fair,
The home of Even's dewy star:
For all were his—o'er earth and sea
His flag had wav'd in Victory,
From proud Himala's realms of snow
To where upon the ocean-tide
Fair Lunka smiles in beauty's glow
And breathes soft perfumes far and wide,
And sits her like a regal maid
In her gay, bridal wreathes array'd!

"A prouder scene the fiery sun
Had never, never shone upon!
Like golden clouds that on the breast
Of yonder Heavens love to rest,
Unnumber'd hosts in bright array
Glitter'd beneath the noon-tide ray;
A thousand flags wav'd on the air,
Like bright-wing'd birds disporting there;
A thousand spears flash'd in the light
In dazzling splendour high and bright.
The warrior-steed so fierce and proud
Neigh'd in wild fury shrill and loud.
The jewell'd elephant too stood
In solemn pride and quiet mood;
And in the glittering pomp of war
The mail-clad hero in his car.
For nations on that glorious day
Met there from regions far away—
The mightiest on this earth that be
In all the pride of Chivalrie—
To celebrate thy feast, proud Victory!

"And all around the dazzled eye
Met scenes of gayest revelrie:
For, here beneath the perfum'd shade,
By some bright silken awning made,

Midst rose and lily scatter'd round
That blush'd as if on fairy ground,
Bright maidens fair as those above
Sang softly—for they sang of Love.

* * * *

"But there was one—a monarch he—
Came not to that high revelrie :
They said he once had sought to gain
That chieftain's daughter but in vain ;
And that his slighted love had taught
Hate, deathless, deep and unforgot :
Such as the bosom's inmost core
Will darkly nurse for ever-more :
Such as will ever fiercely blight
Love, Friendship, Mercy—all that's bright
And gilds Life's path with starry light,
And parts but with the latest breath
That heaves the breast embrac'd by Death !
Perchance this was a whisper'd lie—
An idle tale—foul calumny.
Yet—tho' Inquiry all around
Breath'd from each hurried look and sound—
'Why comes he not ?—once in this hall,
'Now gay with blithesome festival,
'How oft he came—a welcome guest,
'Best lov'd—best cherish'd—honour'd best ?'
Calm was that chieftain's brow and stern
From which conjecture naught could learn :
Yes—calm it was as is the grave
Or some unruffl'd slumbering wave.

"But suddenly a warrior shell
In loud defiance rose and fell ;
As if the Thunderer from on high,
To crush vain mortals met below,

In pomp and grandeur which might vie
With realms above the starry sky,
Came there to work fierce scenes of woe !
And loud it swell'd and hall and bower,
And turret high and skiey tower
Shook, for it was the call to war,
Wild, fierce, and rolling from afar !
The maiden's blushing cheek was pale,
And hush'd her lover's whisper'd tale ;
The hand which strung the breathing lyre,
Seiz'd falchions, bright as blazing fire ;
And thousands from that blithesome hall,
Rush'd madly forth to slay or fall !
Loud was the trumpet's shrilly yell,
And loud the warrior's deafening shell,
And madden'd war-steed's whirl-wind tread,
Which crush'd the dying and the dead !
As when within the starless gloom,
Of Himalaya's snowy womb,
Ten thousand torrents madly roll,
To burst from out its dark control ;
They roar, as if each furious wave,
Writhed wild with life some Fury gave ! "

The tale of the troubadour recited to the guards was heard by the captive princess to rescue whom the singer, in reality the King of Delhi in disguise, had thus made known his mission and identity. They managed to escape together in the night following the recital. The second Canto opens with the Moslem siege of Delhi.

High in his tent of costliest shawl,
Which tow'rs midst thousands, glittering all,
Like fair pavilions Fancy's eyes
View limn'd on sun-set eastern skies,
The Moslem-chief holds glad divan,
Nor fasts and lists to alcoran,

And that grim brow where bigot zeal
Oft set its sternest, fiercest seal,
Smiles gayly like a lightless stream,
When Chandra sheds her silver beam,
As sweetly sounds the gay Sittar,
Like voice of Home when heard afar,
Or wild and thrilling rolls along,
Ferdousi's high, heroic song ;
For ceaseless orison and fast,
Have won Heaven's favouring smile at last,
And when to-morrow's sun shall rise,
On car of light from orient skies,
The first, faint blushing of his ray,
Will lead proud Conquest to her prey,
And see the Crescent's blood-red wave,
Gild fall'n Husteena's lowly grave !

A thousand lamps all gayly shine,
Along the wide extended line ;
And loud the laugh and proud the boast,
Swells from that fierce, unnumber'd host,
And wild the prayer ascends on high,
Dark Vengeance ! thine impatient cry—
"Oh ! for a glimpse of Day's fair brow,
To crush yon city tow'ring now,
To make each cafir-bosom feel,
Th' unerring blade of Moslem steel !
By Alla ! how I long to be,
Where myriads writhe in agony,
And mark each wretch with rolling eye
Call on false gods,—then curse and die,
Meet pilgrim for the dire domain,
Where Eblis holds his sun-less reign !
To-morrow—oh !—why wilt thou, Night,
Thus veil the smile of Day so bright ?

We want not now thy Moon and Star,
In pensive beauty shrin'd afar,
We want not now thy pearly dew
To dim our falchion's blood-red hue,
Thy lonely breath thus passing by,
Like Beauty's whispered, farewell-sigh :
Go—hie thee hence !—where Rocnabad,
With murmuring waters wildly glad,
Doth woo thy stars to silver rest,
Upon its gently-heaving breast,
Or, where soon as the sun hath set,
And dome, kiosk and minaret
Glow with thy pale moon's gentler beam,
Like the bright limnings of some dream,
The lover gayly tunes his lay—
The rosy bow'rs of Mosellay !
We want thee not, the brightest flood,
The fiery sun can ever shed,
Must blaze o'er warrior's deeds of blood,
And light him on whene'er he tread,
The field where foe-men fierce and brave,
Meet, slay, or win a bloody grave ! "

At this point the poem reaches its dramatic climax, and is full of fine feeling for the incidents related. The besieged monarch, the troubadour of the first canto, knows his doom, and goes to break it to his love :—

" Oh ! hast thou conquer'd—have they fled,
And is he come,—and are they dead ?
My God—but why that hueless cheek,
Must Victory thus to true Love speak !
Oh ! tell me, for thy tale must be
Of Joy since thou art come to me !
For fearful visions in my sleep,
Have made me shudder, shriek, and weep !

When wearied with long vigils kept,
I laid me down and thought I slept :
Methought there came a warrior-maid,
With blood-stain'd brow and sheathless blade ;
Dark was her hue, as darkest cloud,
Which comes the Moon's fair face to shroud,
And 'round her waist a hideous zone
Of hands with charnal lightnings shone,
And long the garland which she wore
Of heads all bath'd in streaming gore :
How fierce the eyes by Death unseal'd,
And blasting gleams which they reveal'd.
I shudder'd—tho' I knew 'twas she,
The awful, ruthless Deity,
On whose dread altar like a flood,
There flows for aye her victim's blood !
I shudder'd—for, methought, she came,
With eyes of bright consuming flame,
'Daughter,'—she said,—'farewell !—I go :
'The time is come,—it must be so :
'Leave thee and thine I will to-night,'—
Then vanish'd like a flash of light !

"Again I dreamt :—I saw a pyre
Blaze high with fiercely gleaming fire ;
And one there came,—a warrior he,—
Tho' faint, yet bold,—undauntedly,
And plung'd—oh ! God ! into the flame
Which like a hungry monster rose,
And circl'd round his quivering frame,
A hideous curtain waving close !
I shriek'd—but, tell me why that start,
And paler brow and heaving heart ?
Oh ! tell me, hath my royal sire
Forgot his deep and ruthless ire,
And come and crush'd our foe-men dire ?"

It was the refusal on the part of the monarch who celebrated the Feast of Victory, to come to the rescue of his brother king that enabled the Moslem to triumph. The besieged sovereign implores his lady to fly. She answers in the spirit of ancient Hindu chivalry :—

Oh ! never,—never will this heart
Be sever'd, Love ! to beat apart !
I fear not Death, tho' fierce he be,
When thus I cling, mine own to thee !
For in the forest's green retreat,
Where leafy branches twine and meet,
Tho' wildly round dread Agni roars,
Like angry surge by rock-girt shores,
The soft gazelle of liquid eye
Leaves not her mate alone to die !

The funeral pyre consumes the lovers, and the tale ends with the disappointed Moslem's entry into the doomed city.

High flames the fiercely kindling pyre
Like Rudra's all consuming ire ;
And many a spark ascends on high
Like light-wing'd birds which wildly fly
Or gayly sweep along the sky ;
The Rishi with his gods is there
But weeps as swells his solemn pray'r,
And all around the brightening glow
Lights hueless cheek and pallid brow !
And there be murmured voice of wail,
Like mournful sigh of mid-night gale,
'And must he die so young, so brave,
'Is there no god above to save !'

There is a hush :—a warrior stands
Fast by that pyre of blazing brands ;
With all a warrior's fearless pride
He shrinks not from the fiery tide,

Which rolls, a golden lava-stream,
And darts full many a lightning beam ;
A glittering crown is on his brow
Of beauty,—tho' all pallid now,
And in his hand a broken blade
Bath'd in red gore but lately shed !
He looks him round with dauntless eye,
As one who never fears to die !
'Farewell !—Death's but a short-liv'd pain,
'I Live not for a captive's chain ;
'And now, ye gods who love the brave,
'Smile o'er a warrior's fiery grave !'
He paus'd—they look'd—' oh ! he is gone,
'His last, his boldest deed is done,
'Husteena see thy hope expire,
'Upon yon pile of blazing fire !'

But, hark ! there is a shriek,—a cry,
Of wild, controlless agony !
How fearfully around it rung,
As one burst thro' that weeping throng,
And plung'd into that flaming pyre,
And clove awhile the column'd fire !
They look'd—they knew—yes, it was she,
The bride of him whose spirit there
Had burst its prison, joyously
To fly far to the realms of air !

Go,—ope the portals far and wide,
And let the over-whelming tide
Of foe-men like an ocean glide ;
What boots it now, since they must sheathe
Their blades in hearts have ceas'd to breathe,
And Conquest in proud triumph tread
A lone, wide city of the dead !

Sonnets.

I.

I am not rich, nay, nor the future heir
To sparkling gold or silver heaped on store ;
There is no marble blushing on my floor
With thousand varied dies :—no gilded chair,
No cushions, carpets that by riches are
Brought from the Persian land, or Turkish shore ;
There is no menial waiting at my door
Attentive to the knell : and all things rare,
Born in remotest regions, that shine in
And grace the rich-man's hall, are wanting here.
These are not things that by blind Fate have been
Allotted ever to the poor man's share :
These are not things, these eyes have ever seen,
Tho' their proud names have sounded in this ear !

II.

But oh ! I grieve not ;—for the azure sky
With all its host of stars that brightly shine,
The green-robed earth with all her flow'rs divine,
The verdant vales and every mountain high,
Those beauteous meads that now do glittering lie
Clad in bright sun-shine,—all, oh ! all are mine !
And much there is on which my ear and eye
Can feast luxurious !—why should I repine ?
The furious Gale that howls and fiercely blows,
The gentler Breeze that sings with tranquil glee,
The silver Rill that gayly warbling flows,
And e'en the dark and ever-lasting Sea,
All, all these bring oblivion for my woes,
And all these have transcendent charms for me !

HUR CHUNDER DUTT,
1831–1901.

Tarra Baee.

"Sootan being deprived of Thoda by Lilla the Afghan, occupied Bednore. His daughter Tarra Baee, or the Star of Bednore, stimulated by the reverses of her family, and by the incentive of its ancient glory, scorned the habiliments and occupations of her sex, and devoted herself to manly sports and exercises. When princes made proposals for her hand, her answer was 'Redeem Thoda and my hand is thine.'"

She sat upon her palfrey white,
  That damsel fair and young,
And from the jewelled belt she wore,
  Her trusty rapier hung ;
And chieftains bold, and warriors proud,
Around her formed a gallant crowd.

A helmet clasped her forehead fair,
  A shield was by her side ;
The helmet was of polished steel,
  The shield of bison's hide ;
And as she spoke, the evening air
Disported with her raven hair.

'From girlhood, I have shunned the sports
  In which our sex delight,
And learnt instead to use the sword,
  And wield the falchion bright ;
To meet the tigress turned to bay,
And guide the war-horse in the fray.

'From girlhood, I have vowed a vow
  Our honour to redeem,

And make my noble father's name
  Of every song the theme ;
To rescue Thoda from the slave
Who lives to fill a coward's grave.

'And till my life-blood's purple flow
  Stand stagnant in my veins,
That early vow to see fulfilled
  I'll spare nor strength nor pains :
To those who join me in the war
I'll be a radiant beacon star !

'My hand—'tis his who foremost scales
  The ramparts of the foe,
And to the wicked Lilla deals
  The dread avenging blow ;
Go, warriors—these alone decide
The man who wins me as his bride.'

The Flight of Humayun.

"Humayun fled towards Amarcot. His horse died on the way ; and he desired Tirdi Beg, one of his chiefs, to let him have his horse. The request was refused, so low had royalty fallen. One Koka, dismounting his own mother, gave the king her horse, and placing the lady on a camel ran himself on foot beside her."

At midnight, o'er the desert sands
  The monarch fled alone,
And in the light of paling stars
  His blood-stained armour shone.
Disbanded were his glorious ranks,
  His bravest chieftains slain,
Yet o'er his wide ancestral realm
  Once more he hoped to reign.

The gallant barb which he bestrode
  Had travelled far from home,
And his dun hide on either side
  Was wet with snow-white foam ;
But minding not his toil he sped
  As swiftly as the wind,
To save from foes his regal lord,
  The kindest of the kind.

As horse and horseman onward passed,
  Still feebler waxed the din,
The echoing tramp and deafening shout,
  And roar of culverin.
'Thou bear'st me well, my barb,' he said
  'Thou bear'st me well this night
And I with jewelled bit and band
  Thy labours will requite.'

But ere another hour had passed,
  Down falls the noble steed ;
The king dismounts in fear and haste
  And looks at him with heed,—
Distended nostrils, starting eyes
  And stiffening limbs display
That life with him is ebbing fast
  And soon shall pass away.

Beyond the hills by cloudlets ribbed,
  The broad-disked moon appears,
And o'er the vasty sea of sand
  Its crest of fire uprears ;
And far adown the glimmering glen
  Advance with headlong haste
A hundred fugitives to seek
  The refuge of the waste.

And Tirdi Beg, the veteran chief,
  Among the troop was found,
The king accosted him by name,
  But looked he not around ;
He plied amain his blood-stained spurs
  And passed his lord with speed,—
Thus e'er the cringing race behave
  When most their aid we need.

'Is it for this that from thy youth
  I reared thee in my hall,
And favours heaped on thee and thine
  From which ye feared no fall ?
Is this the guerdon of my love
  So equable and true ?
This night, ungrateful Tirdi Beg,
  This night thou'lt dearly rue.'

'Ho ! Tirdi Beg,' brave Koka cried,
  'Death light upon thy head,
Dost thou desert at utmost need
  Him at whose board thou'st fed ?
The flashing brand that's in my hand
  Shall cleave thy skull in twain,
If e'er upon the tented field
  I meet thee once again.'

'My lord, my king, accept I pray
  A subject's proferred love,
Who, though despised at camp and court,
  Disloyal ne'er shall prove ;
The steed that bore my mother safe,
  Is at my king's command,
And she upon a camel fleet
  Shall cross the sea of sand.

'The foe, the foe, I hear the drum,
The trumpet's echoing peal,
I see the waving of their flags,
The flashing of their steel.
A thousand dark plumes cloud the air,
A thousand flambeaux burn ;
They speed, like eagles from their home,
Among the mountain fern.

'The earth shakes 'neath their chargers' tramp,
Mount, mount my liege in haste,
Ere like the wild and fierce Simoom
They sweep across the waste.
Where Tatta's mountains lift to heaven
Their diadems of snow,
Once more to rear thy banner high
Great king ! we now must go.'

The borrowed steed, with lightning speed,
Forth darts into the wind,
The camel fleet brave Koka leads,
And follows close behind ;
And many a hairbreadth 'scape they made
And trying toil o'ercame,
Till Tatta's lordly mountain peaks
Burst forth in garbs of flame.

And when, again, by heaven's decree
He won his father's throne,
He bade the heralds to proclaim
The deeds by Koka done ;
Jewels and gold—his royal robe,
And lordly 'states he gave
To him who perilled his own life
His monarch's life to save.

Akbar's Dying Charge.

This is no time to weep, my son,
By weeping you do wrong,
But bear thee up right manfully
And in God's love be strong.

Lovely and large thy heritage,
As lovely as a bride,
To keep her still thine own gird on
That bright sword by thy side.

See now it hangs on yonder wall
(For powerless is the hand
That wielded it in hunt or fray)
My own, my noble brand.

Read what is writ on either side
And write it in your breast,
Those characters of gold shine clear :
'The merciful are blest.'

Upon the jewelled hilt and haft
The diamond-sparks bespeak
The grasp around it must be pure
Though not infirm or weak.

At honour's beck, in kingdom's cause,
Like lightning let it fall,
With power avenge the oppressed and wronged,
And justly rule o'er all.

The blood-stains on the polished steel
At mercy's fount make clean,
And may thy battle-fields right soon
With waving crops be green.

In all the triumphs, all the joys
  Which thy good angel brings,
Forget not to give glory, son,
  To God the King of kings.

His blessing crave, his grace implore,
  Alike in weal and woe,
Long be thy reign in this fair land,—
  I go where all things go.

Sonnet.

INDIA.

O yes ! I love thee with a boundless love,
Land of my birth ; and while I lisp thy name,
Burns in my soul ' an Aetna of pure flame '
Which none can quench nor aught on earth remove.
Back from the shrouded past, as with a spell,
Thy days of glory memory recalls,
And castles rise, and towers, and flanking walls,
And soldiers live, for thee dear land who fell ;
But as from dreams of bliss men wake to mourn,
So mourn I when that vision is no more,
And in poor lays thy widowed fate deplore,
Thy trophies gone, thy beauteous laurels torn,
But Time shall yet be mocked ;—though these decay,
I see broad streaks of a still brighter day.

The Rakhi.

Wear, wear this fillet round thy arm,
  Thou brave and noble knight,
Thy gallant warhorse paws the ground,
  Impatient for the fight.

A sister's love for thee hath wrought
  This silken tie so fair,
That thou protected by the gods
  The deadly fray may'st share.

Thy flashing eyes full plainly tell
  Thou'lt not disgrace the band,
If e'er the impetuous tide of war
  Roll where thy loved ones stand.

And sheath not, knight, thy gleaming blade,
  Till routed is the foe ;
And as the chaff before the wind,
  Before thy ranks they go.

And when by glorious Victory crowned
  Thou tread'st the bloody field,
Spare, by my tears, the wounded foe ;
  Be thou their help and shield.

But hark ! the tocsin's quivering peal
  Bursts on my ear from far—
Mount, mount thy steed that proudly neighs
  To join the ranks of war.

GOVIN CHUNDER DUTT,
1828–1884.

Song from the Bengali.

Oh, never look on woman's eyes !
  Their serpent gaze will fascinate
And then betray thee ; youth, be wise
  And fly their lustre ere too late ;
Or shouldst thou linger, loth to part,
  Oh, never, never trust her heart !

Oh, never list to woman's voice !
  There's flattery in its every tone
To make thy pulses throb, rejoice,
  And leave thee then to mourn alone ;
But shouldst thou linger, loth to part,
  Oh, never, never trust her heart !

Oh, never let thy bosom heave
  For woman's twin-born blush and smile !
The glittering smile will oft deceive,
  The blush, alas ! as oft beguile ;
But shouldst thou linger, loth to part,
  Oh, never, never trust her heart !

To Lord Canning.

Though a thousand pens condemned thee, mine still should
  write thy praise ;
Though a thousand tongues reviled thee, mine still should
  pæans raise ;
For factious clamours heeding not, that only call for blood,
True to thy duty and thy race, Lord Canning, thou hast stood.

What is the meed of thy deserts? Let history blush to tell!
A foul memorial of recall sent o'er the ocean's swell;
And from the press—a press, alas! long held in honour too—
The daily sneer for justice done, as God hath taught to do!

Is this the meed of thy deserts? No, no, it cannot be!
All England's best and noblest are heart and soul with thee!
And India's swarthy children, from hill and field and town,
Lift up the voice with one acclaim, and blessings summon down.

And the next age—shall it not hear, with wonder and with awe,
How amidst rancour, hate, and strife, thou sternly gavest law?
'He governed all alike'—'twill say—'all races and all creeds,
He judged not men by skin or faith, he judged them by their deeds.'

And the next life? Is there not one when God shall judge us all,
The peasant from his cottage and the ruler from his hall?
Then who shall justified appear, and who shall win the crown?
The man that strove for duty, or the man that sought renown?

All that a bold wise heart can do—all that a righteous may,
Was done the bursting storm to quell in India's evil day!
But a heavy task is still on hand, for an omniscient God
Hath women's blood and children's seen run reeking on the sod.

Yes, a heavy task remains behind— a burden's laid on thee,
Thou hast been chosen Minister—such is thy destiny;
Oh, pray—for highest counsel pray!—of such shalt thou have need,
For vengeance is a fearful thing—and vengeance is decreed.

Strike thou and home, but not in wrath fulfil a high command ;
Avenging angels weep to smite a sin-o'erburdened land ;
Strike, mourning, at the word of God, and hold at His behest
These words in water are not writ—'The merciful are blest.'

It is not for her trampled flag that England bares her sword ;
It is not for a just revenge upon a murderous horde ;
It is to prove to blood-stained men, self-blinded of their sight,
That evil hath no chance with good or darkness with the light.

But guiltless blood, where'er it flows, in black or white men's veins
Is precious in the sight of Him who trieth heart and reins ;
Oh, watch it be not shed in vain !—Oh, act as heretofore !
And let a wreath-encircled name one priceless wreath have more.

A Farewell To Romance.

Farewell !—a long farewell—to thee, Romance !
We may not meet as we have met before,
Though yet the witchery of that downcast glance
Enthralls my heart, it must enthral no more.
Though yet the music of thy silver voice
Rings in my ear—it must no longer ring ;
The stern command of duty bids us part,
The moments hasten and she grants us few ;
But ere thou speed'st where younger hearts rejoice,
And ere I wander like an alien thing,
Jostling and jostled in the world's wide mart,
Fain would I murmur 'mid my sighs ' Adieu.'

Who hath not seen thee, fair one, when the day
  Urges his coursers o'er the dappled clouds,
Flit o'er the dewsprent lawns in green array ?
  Who hath not seen thee when the evening shrouds
The landscape hushed, by skirt of forest wide,
  Listening transfixed to echoes floating there,
    Pale as a statue and as motionless ;
      Or kneeling by the margin of a stream,
Wherein thine image might be dimly spied,
  While the winds dallied with thy bosom bare,
    And raised thy robes, and oft in wantonness
      Rippled thy mirror, to destroy thy dream ?

Who hath not seen thee in his chamber still
  At dead of night ? For me, I've seen thee oft,
When through the lattice came the moonlight chill,
  With incense from the garden borne aloft.
The star of peace flamed ever on thy brow
  Just where the hair was parted, and thy face,
    That pale and pensive face, was aye serene
      As a white lotus on its watery throne :
One hand upheld a verdant cypress bough,
  The other on thy lip with artless grace
    A finger pressed—while o'er thy head was seen,
      Round yet apart, a rainbow-tinted zone.

Yes, I have seen thee many and many a night,
  But silent ever, and thine eyes have made
(Those eyes where quiver passion's tear drops bright)
  A deep impression on my heart, and laid
A spell upon me that I may not rend—
  A spell that half unfits me for the strife
    Recurring constant in the work-day world.
      Ah ! how I long to linger by thy side

In pathless wilds, where leafy branches bend
Each above each—the busy hum of life
Is never felt—the contest-flag is furled,
And from his foes the wounded deer may hide.

It may not be ; I dare not disobey
The trumpet-voice of duty which I hear,
With aching bosom, call me hence away,
And bid me leave thee whom I love so dear.
Therefore farewell—a long farewell—Romance !
We may not meet as we have met before,
For now my leisure hours can be but few.
Yet when we meet what raptures shall there be,
Upon some rare, rare holiday, by chance,
Roving in gardens as I roved of yore
At evening, when the stars begem the blue,
And warbling birds awake to ecstasy.

And if we meet not—if thou shunn'st my sight,
Scared at my world-worn brow and haggard look,
Then shall I woo thee with the charms of might,
And pore intently on some well-loved book—
Well-loved of old, to be well-loved no more—
The varied melody of Shakespeare's shell,
The Doric flute of Milton, or the reed
Of 'sage and serious' Spenser ever dear,
In breathless silence heard so oft before
By thee and me, (thou did'st confess the spell ;)
Or what less deep, of late, thou lov'st to hear
The strains of Scott that stir the soul indeed.

If time or care thine image should efface,
The image deeply graven on my brain,
And scenes seem dull which once I loved to trace,
And books, once prized, afford no balm to pain,

Where shall I seek to light the fire anew ?
How find thee, Goddess of the peerless eyes ?
In mine own hearth, and in the prattle sweet
Of children dear, and in their sunny glance,
And in their love so tender and so true,
A love that every morning magnifies.
Though parting now, we thus may sometime meet
And love each other as of old, Romance.

Lines.

When from the dewsprent rose the blustering wind
Steals leaf by leaf away,
Sighs the sad flower to leave no trace behind,
No record of its day ?

When the fair colours in the rainbow laid,
Dissolve in heaven's own hue,
Weep they to find their glories blend and fade
Into the pristine blue ?

When stars on stars before the rising sun
Sink down and disappear,
Mourns any that its brief career is run,
And leaves no vestige here ?

Why then should man alone indulge in grief,
Or ever wish to give
A frail memorial of his sojourn brief
To those who later live ?

What the necessity of earthly fame,
Or monument, or mound,
To one who in the Book of Life, his name
Shall see, if faithful found ?

Wordsworth's Poems.

This volume is a Gothic church—no less,
And every separate poem but a part
Of a great edifice, built with rarest art,
A cell, or oratory, or carved recess,
Or but a simple leaf-wreath winding round
A marble pillar, in the sombre light,
Or an emblazoned window flashing bright,
Fair in itself, but fairest where 'tis found ;
Each delicately symmetrical—but the whole
Ravishing with loveliness the prisoned soul.

The labour of a lifetime, and the work
Of one inspired, the prophet of his age.
What deep philosophy and experience sage
And tender sympathies here retired lurk
In simplest verses. Oh, beloved book !
With thee and but one other, which to name
Even with thee would matter be for blame,
Contented could I glide o'er life's calm brook,
Until it mingle with the mighty sea,
And time be swallowed in eternity.

Nor deem this praise extravagant or strange,
For without travel here I have its joys,
And sitting by my hearth where naught annoys,
O'er hills and oceans by these spells I range.
Is it not grand to see Helvellyn rear
Its lofty summit to the azure sky,
Or mark the lake below faint-gleaming lie,
A mirror for all objects far and near,
Bare rocks, and woods arrayed in vivid green,
And cheerful homesteads through the foliage seen ?

And should an English landscape ever pall,
  With all its wide diversity of hills
  And trees and waters, lo ! the fresh breeze fills
Our swelling canvas at the Poet's call !
Where shall we wander ? In the fields of France ?
  Or classic Italy's wave-saluted shore ?
  Or dearer Scotland's barren heaths and moor ?
Or Staffa's natural temple, where in trance
We shadowy beings may behold ? Command,—
All wait the movement of the enchanter's wand.

Hail, ye Rydalian laurels that have grown
  Untended by the Poet's calm abode,
  And in the footpaths that he often trod
Wrapt in deep thought, at evening time, alone.
No Delphic wreath he wanted, when he found
  Nature unveiled in all her loveliness,
  But these wild leaves and wilder flowers that bless
Our common earth he prayed for, and she bound
His brows therewith ; and see, they never fade,
A crown of amaranth by her own hands made.

Home.

No picture from the master hand
  Of Gainsborough or Cuyp may vie
With that which at my soul's command
  Appears before mine inward eye
In foreign climes when doomed to roam—
Its scene, my own dear native home.

What though no cloud-like hills uprear
  Their serried heights sublime afar !
What though the ocean be not near,
  With wave and wind in constant war !

Nor rock nor sea could add a grace,
So perfect seems the hallowed place.

Casuarinas in solemn range,
At distance look like verdant hills ;
And winds draw from them music strange,
Such as the tide makes when it fills
Some shingle-strown and land-girt bay
From men and cities far away.

And round, as far as eye can reach
What vivid piles of foliage green !
Mango and shaddock, plum and peach,
And palms like pillars tall between :
An emerald sea surrounds the nest,
A sea for ever charmed in rest.

What roses blossom on the lawn !
What warblers on the bamboo boughs,
Lithe and elastic, swing at dawn,
And pour their orisons and vows !
What dew upon the greensward lies !
How lovingly look down the skies !

And at high noon when every tree
Stands brooding on its round of shade,
And cattle to the shelter flee
And there, in groups recumbent laid,
Gaze ruminant—what deep repose
Lies on the landscape as it glows !

But most at evening's gentle hour
The reign of Peace is clearly read,
In the blue mists which hail her power,
Pavilions rich and banners spread,
While 'mid the hush is heard the tone
Of night's sweet minstrel—hers alone.

As star by star leaps out above,
  As twilight deepens into night,
As round me cluster those I love,
  And eye meets eye in glances bright,
I feel that earth itself may be
Lit up with heaven's own radiancy.

Night on the Ganges.

How beautiful the glorious night would be,
How much more lovely than the garish day,
If thus for ever she arrayed herself !
The moon is up—high on the cloudless sky,
Over the towering mast she brightly gleams,
Pale, like a lady sick with silent grief,
Showering her beams on everything around,
And clear defining every rope and spar
Of this our gallant bark, whose shadow falls
Enormous, on the smooth reflecting wave.
In this pure light the eye with ease discerns
Each distant object that it sees by day,
And freed from every fault that sunbeams show.
It seems, indeed, a clear meridian noon
Reft of its heat, its turmoil, and its strife,
Its busy wasting cares, its stunning noise,
Its idle flouting glare, and scorching winds.
Naught now disturbs the stillness of the scene—
The holy stillness—save the cricket's song
That lulls each weary sense to pleasant sleep
By shrill monotony, and the night-bird's lay.
Anon that lay is hushed. The fishes leap
Up in the clear moonlight from out the wave,
Then fall again and raise a sullen splash ;
The huge unwieldy porpoise rolling out,

Sinks down immediate. Sudden from the glade,
A spectral, hollow, long-repeated cry
Of wild ducks in alarm comes loud and shrill,
Blent with the famished jackal's harsher voice,
As ruthlessly that tyrant's steps pursue
These harmless dwellers of the tangled brakes.
Soft spread the dews upon the fragrant earth,
Beading with orient pearls the silken grass,
And emerald leaves of trees upon the banks
That bound with green the dim horizon's verge,
On every side, save that in which the stream
Loses itself amid the bending sky.
How pleasant now, at ease reclined to mark
The sombre shadows of each varying tree :
The mangoe here, with countless leaves adorned,
Casts densest shade, and there the towering palm
Mirrors its length. The scented baubool next
With fragrant yellow flowers and clust'ring leaves,
Bends o'er the wave to see its image fair.
One mass of green the trees far off appear,
And cast new shadows on the flood below.
The ample Ghaut its thousand pillars rears
In the dim moonshine, looking vast and pale,
Untenanted and cold, sublimely grand ;
And the high temple with its upward points,
Shaded by moonlight like a phantom, looms
In dim mysterious beauty. At this time,
The spirit of eternal peace seems thrown
On every object, and the rudest breast
Is filled with pure and unimpassioned thoughts.
May such a calmness in my dying hour
Encircle me, while those I dearly love
Stand by—not mourning—and may my passing soul
Partake in that mysterious, awful time
The peace and stillness of the scene around.

OMESH CHUNDER DUTT,
1836–1912.

The Chief of Pokurna.

Within the merry greenwood,
  At dawning of the day,
Four-and-twenty armed men
  In silent ambush lay.
They wait like couchant leopards,
  Their eager eyes they strain,
And look towards the lonely glade,
  Towards the distant plain.
Naught see they but the golden corn
  Slow waving in the sun,
Naught see they but the misty hills
  And uplands bare and dun.
The rustle of the forest leaves,
  The trampling of the deer,
The chirp of birds upon the boughs,
  Are all the sounds they hear.

But hark ! they catch the thrilling notes
  Of a distant bugle horn
Come pealing through the wild ravine,
  By the morning breezes borne :
Lower they stooped, and anxiously
  Their laboured breath they drew,
And clutched their brands with nervous hands—
  Their quarry is in view,
Attended by a single squire,
  Slow riding up the glen,

Unconscious that his path's beset
  By armed and desperate men ;
A brave gerfalcon on his wrist,
  The bugle on his breast,
The sunlight gleaming brightly on
  His nodding plume and crest.

Not clad in steel, from head to heel
  In satin rich arrayed,
With his trusty sword, Pokurna's lord
  Is riding through the glade,
To see his falcon proudly soar
  And strike, he comes so far ;
In peaceful guise he rideth on,
  Nor dreams of blood or war.
All sudden from their ambush
  The treacherous foemen rose,
With vengeful eyes and glittering arms,
  With spears and bended bows :
And ere the chief could draw his blade,
  They hemmed him darkly round,
And plucked him from his frightened steed,
  And bore him to the ground.

The king sat on a gorgeous throne,
  All rough with ruddy gold,
Begirt with many a haughty peer,
  And warriors stern and bold ;
With many a vassal-prince around,
  For they had come from far
To pay their homage to their lord,
  The sovereign of Marwar.
With fetters on his manly hands,
  Within that hostile ring,
With dauntless look the chief appeared
  Before his angry king.

For he had often vaunted thus,
  In public and alone,
'Within my dagger's sheath I hold
  This kingdom's royal throne.'

Before his angry king he stood,
  The king he had defied,
Nor quailed he 'neath that princely glance
  Nor vailed his brow of pride ;
Though bent on him were fiery eyes,
  And looks of rage and hate,
He stood as calm as if he were
  Within his castle gate.
The monarch spoke, his words rang out
  In accents stern and clear,
'Ha ! traitor, insolent and keen,
  At last we have thee here ;
Where now are all thy boastings vain,
  Amidst thy men of war ?
Say, where is now the sheath which holds
  The fortunes of Marwar ?'

Oh ! grimly turned Pokurna's lord,
  And loud and long laughed he,
Then waved his hand towards the prince
  And answered loftily :
'I left it with my gallant son,
  Within Pokurna's hall ;
Tremble, false prince, for sure he will
  Avenge his father's fall !'
The monarch's swarthy cheeks grew pale,
  The lightning filled his eye :
'And dar'st thou, rebel, even here,
  Thy sovereign lord defy ?
Ho, soldiers ! drag the traitor out,
  And ere the close of day

Let his foul carcase feed the dogs
  Upon the public way.'

Oh ! gaily in a golden shower
  The setting sunlight falls
Upon the waste of glinting sand
  Which girds Pokurna's walls.
The warder paced the battlements,
  With heavy steps and slow,
And from within arose a cry,
  A wail of grief and woe.
There noble dames shed heart-wrung tears,
  And rent their glossy hair,
And cried aloud for him, the dead,
  And beat their bosoms bare.
And cursed with bitter, bitter words
  The prince at whose command
Was foully slain their noble chief,
  The bravest in the land.

Far different was the scene within
  That castle's ancient hall,
Where, 'neath the glorious banners
  Which graced the blackened wall,
Five hundred mailed warriors
  And chiefs of high emprise
Around their youthful leader stood,
  With stern yet moistened eyes.
They bared at once their shining blades
  And lifted them on high,
And swore a deep and deadly oath
  To avenge their lord or die.
Full well their solemn oath they kept
  In many a mortal fray,
And sorely rued that haughty prince
  The deed he did that day.

The Hindu Wife to her Husband.

"An English lady, visiting an odalisque, inquired what pleasure her profusion of rich ornaments could afford, as no person except her husband was ever to behold them. 'And for whom,' replied the fair oriental, 'do you adorn yourself?—is it for other men?'"

Oh, not for strangers do I wear
The jewels in my flowing hair,
Nor yet for others' eyes array
My limbs in vestments rich and gay:
Nor wish that even friends should see
The smile that's only meant for thee.

From pleasures of this life debarred,
They tell me that my lot is hard,
That, forc'd like prison'd bird to pine,
Such joys as theirs can ne'er be mine;
That beauty, wit, and gems are vain
If hidden they must thus remain.

They tell me that in festal hall,
To be admired and prais'd by all,
To feel one's self—O triumph high!—
The cynosure of every eye,
The fairest of the fair to be:
This, this is life,—bright, glad and free.

From such advice I turn away,
It only serves to lead astray:
The dance, the crowd, are not for me,
I envy not their liberty:—
Happy as queen upon her throne,
I love to dwell among mine own.

Is there no peace for them at home,
That restless here and there they roam?
And are they of their lords so tired,
That they should seek to be admired

By friends and strangers? Thus can they
Mid dance, and song, and jest, be gay?

For thee alone, my love, I wear
The jewels in my flowing hair,
For thee the glance, for thee the smile,
For thee this heart which knows no guile:
And blest, supremely blest I'll be
With one kind word and look from thee.

Hymn to Shiva.

Shiva! whom all the gods in heaven obey,
Thou mightiest, deign to hear my humble prayer!
I've sinned. Oh, save me from the fiend Despair,
Which turns to gloom the sunshine of the day!
The angry storms of Fate around me play,
Strange sounds are hurtling through the troubled air,
Be thou my steadfast rock, my guide, and stay.

Thou who art king of all the things I see,
Thou who art clothed in glory and in light,
Thou from whose tresses sprang, in radiance bright,
The sacred Ganges rolling wide and free,
Thou art my hope—lo! here I bring to thee,
To find forgiveness in thy awful sight,
These varied offerings on my bended knee.

Dread lord of Uma, to whose golden shrine
In far Benares countless pilgrim bands,
From Indian cities and from distant lands,
Yearly repair in never-ending line,
I too will visit that abode divine,
If I but now receive thy high commands;—
Oh, leave me not in bitter grief to pine!

O thou! who dwellest on the lofty crown
'Mid the pure snows of cloud-capped Kalasay,
From thy bright region of ne'er-ending day,
In pity on this sinful one look down.
Chase from thy lofty brow that angry frown,
And let me go in peace of mind away,
Rejoicing, to my distant native town.

Sonnets—War.

I

How terrible art thou O iron War!
With vengeful furies in thy long-drawn train,
Thy step is found e'en o'er the trackless main,
Nor rock, nor sea thy fiery course can bar.
Where'er thou goest in thy rattling car,
Deserted hamlet and ensanguin'd plain,
Attest thy cruel and tyrannic reign,
And flaming towns gleam lurid from afar.
Thy blood-red standard to the winds display'd,
Thy drum's deep roll, thy trumpets shrill and clear,
The thunder of the furious cannonade,
Are sights and sounds which fill the heart with fear;
For they presage, alas! too well we know,
Rapine and wreck, untimely death and woe.

II.

But yesterday upon this ravaged spot,
Rose the proud city lifting high in air
Its graceful arches and its columns fair,
Here was the mart with life and tumult fraught;
O cruel War, what ruin hast thou wrought!
Outrage and wrong are rampant everywhere:
Hark to those shrieks, wild cry, and hopeless prayer,
Bursting alike from hall and lowly cot!

Is this the glory, this the deathless fame,
  Which thou dost promise to thy lawless crew !
Shall we for this emblazon forth thy name,
  Shall we for this thy path with flowerets strew !
  Away,—tho' proud thy brow, and dark its frown,
It is not worthy of the victor's crown.

Sonnets—Peace.

I.

Come gentle Peace, with Plenty at thy side,
  And scatter with a free and bounteous hand,
  Thy gifts and blessings over all the land.
  The earth has worn the rich robes of a bride,
The trees lift up their stately heads in pride,
  The cloudless skies with varied hues look grand,
  The air is full of perfume sweet and bland,
To welcome thee, O goddess tender-eyed !
We love thee with an ardent love sincere,
  For 'neath thy quiet and benignant sway,
Gaunt Care, and sombre Grief, and trembling Fear
  Depart, and vanish from our homes away,
And sunshine lights each heart so dark erewhile,
The glad bright sunshine of thy cheerful smile.

II.

Lo ! where they stand upon yon village green,
  Youths and young maidens in a joyous round,
  Hark to the violin and pipe's sweet sound,
As they strike up to greet May's lovely queen.
High in the midst the slender pole is seen,
  With garlands bright and prizes gaily crown'd ;
  O, can a fairer sight than this be found,

Where all is mirth, no shadows intervene !
O Peace, our guardian angel, may thy throne
  Be fix'd and steadfast on our fertile shore,
And may we ne'er thy sov'reignty disown,
  But love and worship thee for evermore ;
The crown, the laurel wreath are meet for thee,
Thine is the triumph, thine the victory !

NOBO KISSEN GHOSE (Ram Sharma).
1837–1918.

In Memoriam

MICHAEL MADHUSUDAN DUTT.

Mourn, poor Bangala, mourn, thy hapless state !
Thy swan, thy warbler's snatched by ruthless fate !
Oh, snatched in prime of life, thy darling child,
Datta who sang in magic numbers wild
Great Megnath—Indra's haughty conquering foe,
Hurled by brave Lakshman to the shades below !
—Hushed is the tuneful voice that thrilled the soul,
Silent the lyre whose swelling notes did roll
In streams of music sweet that did impart
A life—a soul ev'n to the dullest heart !
Ah, poor unhappy land ! how sad thy doom,
Thy noblest sons are lost in vigor's bloom !
Oh Death how stern, implacable thou art
To single them out for thy cruel dart !
Ye children of Bangala, o'er his bier
Pour forth your sorrows—shed the grateful tear
To wit and talents due, and genius rare,
Now lost beyond the reach of hope and care !
What though no pageant grand, no funeral show
Followed his hearse in sable garb of woe ?
What though no column high, no living bust
Should mark the spot where lies his honoured dust ?
He needs not these, though prized by little men ;
His works his noblest monument remain !
Oh, crown your poet's grave with flowery wreaths,
The flesh is dead, th' immortal spirit breathes !

Portraits from "The Last Day."

I. LORD CANNING.

And now I see a noble figure cast
In highest beauty's mould, whose lofty brow
Bespeaks a pure and gracious soul within.
He looks the image bright of Clemency ;
And as he moves, lo ! Peace attends his steps.
When a fierce hurricane swept o'er the East,
And men hurled Reason from her tottering throne,
With cheeks unblanched, stout heart, and iron nerves,
He curb'd their passions wild, and firmly check'd
War's blood-hounds in their merciless career,
And thus from ruin saved a classic land,
And fair Humanity from lasting shame.
Oh, baleful days ! whose memory still sends
A thrill of horror through the circling veins !
Oh, stormy days ! when lacerated Peace
Lay all but lifeless upon Mercy's lap,
And Virtue—Innocence—Religion's self,
Like storm-kiss'd flowers, with consternation shook ;
While with infernal merriment, hell laughed
To find another hell produced on earth !
In that dread saturnalia of blood,
This righteous statesman stood revealed in all
His moral grandeur ; violence and rapine
And lawlessness fled at his stern command ;
He brought down Mercy from her heavenly bower,
The sword of Justice tempered with her dew !

II. RAJA RAMMOHAN ROY.

Among that saintly host, with thrilling joy
And pride, I see the bold Reformer, who
In darkest times flung off the yoke of Falsehood ;

And, putting on the panoply of light,
Brought bright-eyed Truth from her secluded home
Amidst Himalaya's eternal snows
Back to his native plain, from whence she had
In terror fled, all scared by hateful rites
Revolting of a hellish superstition.
Filled with the learning of the East and West,
An intellectual Samson in the midst
Of Philistines grovelling in ignorance,
And fallen from their simple ancient faith,
He consecrated, with unflinching zeal,
His mighty mind with all its gifts and powers,
Its wealth of knowledge spoiled from hoary Time,
Its deepest thoughts, and fondest, brightest hopes,
To the sole service of his God and kind.
O! noble life with noble deeds replete!
'Twas thine the glory and the grace and joy
To save thy country's new-born buds from slaughter
On the altars of a fell idolatry,
And widowed female hearts all warm and throbbing
With full-blooded life from off the blazing pyre!
  Thine the still higher glory to erect
God's church pure from abominations foul
On the strong rock of Nature's revelation,
Which ne'er deceiveth, understood aright.

III. DAVID HARE.

  Next see he comes, with smiling looks benign,
The grand old man, who left his sea-girt home
In the far West, to spouse Philanthropy
In fair Bengala's grove of champac bright;
Who fondly, passionately clave to her,
And only her, thro' weal and woe, in health
And sickness, and thro' good report and evil,
Unchanged and changeless with the ceaseless whirl

Of self and passions' bustling stir around!
For he re-lit the lamp of Knowledge, where
Her crystal light had been for ages quenched,
And all his heart and soul and means employed
In serving selflessly an ancient race,
Borne down by wars and robber-hordes, and pining
In the deep gloom of Freedom's longest night.
His life was but a stream of golden deeds,
A white page undefiled by blur or blot;
And so he left a blessed name behind,
A name told on the heart's own rosary.
Methinks I see a merry troop of boys
Gathered round him, the centre of their sports;
And as the fun goes round, loud ringing peals
Of elfin laughter greet each sprightly prank
The little folk—spring-flowers of innocence—
Invent, to speed the joyous hours away.
And he the while views them with glistening eyes,
Or joins them in their sports, more blithe and gay
Than even the merriest, playfullest of them;
Or now and then, as they fall out, decides
Their little suits, and harmony restores.
Blest spirit hallowed be thy name, and cherished
In kind remembrance to the verge of time!

Hymn to Durga.

HAIL Mighty Goddess! Universal Soul!
  Power or Love, Fate or Illusion sweet!
Whate'er thy name, O mother, whose control
  All nature quickens—humbly thee I greet!
Hail! ten-armed Goddess of the lion-throne,
Whose power Time and Space and Being own!
The seed of things was in thy mighty womb,
Their source prolific, and their final doom!

From thee the mystic Trinal Unity—
  Brahma, Vishnu, Mahesha—one in three—
All sprung, thou primal dread Divinity,
  Thou great First Cause of all and End to be !
The wondrous glories of yon azure sky,
The nameless beauties that around us lie,
The whirlwind's blast, and lightning's dazzling flame,
All—all thy pow'r and providence proclaim.

Descend, great Deity ! from thy cloud girt seat
  Amidst the changeless, everlasting snows
Of lofty Himmala, where at thy feet
  Time's self doth lie like Passion in repose.
And Kartikaya on his star-eyed bird,
As fits the war-god, bravely keeps his guard ;
And Ganesha, in sober vesture drest
Wooing Philosophy to his loving breast.

And golden Lakshmee, smiling like the morn,
  And bright as when she rose from the ocean foam,
Her lap adorn'd with golden ears of corn,
  Emparadises still thy mountain home.
And lovely Saraswatee—lute in hand—
Attended by the Arts—a witching band—
Awakes ethereal music midst the snows,
And all the place with rapturous ardour glows.

The Aryan world prepares for social mirth
  By acts of lovingkindness to mankind ;
May universal love pervade the earth,
  And charity fill every heart and mind !
May brother brother clasp in close embrace,
And pleasure beam in each familiar face,
As friend meets friend around the festive board
And tells of pangs endured or triumphs scored !

Come, Mother come, all clothed in holy light,
The sun and moon both shining at thy feet.
O bless our hearths and homes ! O bless our sight
With visions of the glorious Infinite !
In varied names we worship only thee ;
In vain, the creeds veil thee in mystery :
For God or Goddess, it is all the same—
In every form we worship but thy name !

Come, Goddess bright, O come, Supernal Power,
In beaming smiles and loveliness arrayed,
Our only hope in dark misfortune's hour,
Our sole support, and never-failing aid !
O bless the land with Peace and tranquil Joy !
May no distressing ills the Year annoy !
O come with all thy radiant progeny,
Durga, Durga, Durgatinashini !

Robert Knight.

Sudden the Indian sky is overcast,
And all the land is shrouded deep in gloom :
A wail goes forth from many an Indian home,
And tears from old and young are streaming fast.

For where is he, our fearless champion bold,
India's unflinching advocate and friend,
Whose lofty purpose and whose cherish'd end,
Were Justice, Truth, and Righteousness to uphold ?

Alas, the generous soul is now no more !
Hush'd the large heart, whose love our hearts had won !
O noble Knight, thy mortal warfare o'er,
O weary pilgrim thy long journey done,

Rest, from thy loving toil and labour rest,
Repose, in peace on thy Redeemer's breast !

MAHARAJAH SIR JOTINDRA MOHUN TAGORE, 1831–1908.

An Indian Wreath.

Bring **CHAMPA** from the bower,
Fresh blown and of a golden dye ; inweave
Gay **APRAJITA** of the richest blue,
That rivals Beauty's eyes when lit by Love
First dawning. **BELH** too,—sweet **BELA** cull,
That blooms in virgin loveliness serene,
And with it twine ambrosial **JANTI** fair
Whose fragrance well may vie with **PARIJAT**
Of Indra's bower. Forget not **NAGESHUR**,
The Love-God's fav'rite ; for with that he tips
This flowery shaft, and him the world obeys :
With these in clusters bright **ASOKA** braid,
—A charm 'gainst broken hearts and sorrow's pangs,—
And **GUNDHARAJ** that sends its frankincense
Afar ; then gather sweet **SAPHALIKA**,
That blooms and falls at eventide, nor waits
It e'er the Day-God's ardent looks to meet,
Like maids who coyly shun each wanton gaze ;
And **RAJNI-GANDHA**, that expands at night
Alone, and like a lover's vow doth breathe
Its odour rich in secret. There—'tis done,
The wreath's complete, an offering rich and rare,
Fit to adorn the forehead of the fair.

The Rajput Soldier's Farewell.

Adieu ! 'Tis time for me to part
While yet from bondage free,
While yet I may persuade my heart
To bid farewell to thee, dear love ! to bid farewell to thee.

Now sounds the *nagra* loud and deep,
To war it turns my mind,
I go where duty calls, nor weep
To leave thee here behind, dear love ! to leave thee here behind.

Where lazy peace still holds her sway
I cannot now remain,
Nor must I love's soft voice obey
The Rajput name to stain, dear love ! the Rajput name to stain.

Once more farewell ! If gracious *Raam*
But spare this life of mine,
For every pain I'll find a balm
On those sweet lips of thine, dear love ! on those sweet lips of thine.

But if remorseless death should dart
The cruel shaft at me,
Though hence my spirit should depart,
It still should pray for thee, dear love ! it still should pray for thee.

The Gopees' Address to the Kokil.

Ah ! cease, dear Kokil, cease to sing
Thy soft enchanting lays,
For, ever to our minds they bring
The thoughts of happier days, sweet bird !
The thoughts of happier days !

And mem'ry fondly paints the scene,
When in the *Tamal* grove
We joyous danced and struck the *Veen*
And sang of youth and love, sweet bird !
And sang of youth and love !

What time the moonbeams brightly glanced
On yonder flowery mead,
How oft we sat and heard entranced
The BLUE GOD'S distant reed, sweet bird !
The BLUE GOD'S distant reed !

When *Phalgoon* showered her beauties bright,
And bloomed both hearts and flowers,
How joyous then we past the night
In *Jumna's* blessed bowers, sweet bird !
In Jumna's blessed bowers !

But past and gone are those sweet days,
And all our joys are o'er ;
Thy songs but sad remembrance raise,
Oh ! sing thy lays no more, sweet bird !
Oh ! sing thy lays no more !

Origin of the Kaminee Flower.

A maiden fair once loved a youth,
To win his smile she ever sighed,
But false she found his plighted truth,
Of broken heart the maiden died.

The Love-God's breast with pity warmed,
And now for once himself he blamed,
Into a flower the maid transformed,
And sweet *Kaminee* it was named.

And evermore alone at night,
It weeps full many a dewy tear,
But fades and falls ere dawn of light,
Lest faithless man approach it near.

GREECE CHUNDER DUTT.

1833–1892.

The Maid of Roopnagore.

The Emperor Aurungzeb, in the height of his power, made an offer of marriage to the Princess of Roopnagore, who haughtily rejected his suit, saying, that she would rather renounce the throne of her ancestors than be allied to an infidel.

Hear how the maid of Roopnagore
Disdained the friendship of the Moor,
When forth by royal hest there came,
With peers and paladins of fame,
A gay young lordling of degree,
The pride of Moslem chivalry,
To win her from her father's side,
To be a Kaffir sovereign's bride.

'Go back, Sir Knight,' she sternly said,
While maiden shame her cheeks dyed red,
'Go back and say, for gems and gold,
For lordly Delhi's guarded hold,
For power, for state, for lands in fee,
An odalisque I ne'er will be,
Nor faith and troth will coldly sell
To him who is an infidel.

'The dun-deer on the mountain's side
May with the panther be allied;
Compelled by bleak December's weather,
The owl and lark may house together;
Or yet by spring inspired the dove
May seek the hawk's protecting love;
But Roopnagore in weal and woe
Shall ever deem the Moor a foe.

'In rich brocade, and jewels sheen,
Rather than shine the Moslem's queen,
Rather than greet a fratricide,
I'd be a simple shepherd's bride,
And take as readily my share
Of rustic toil and rustic care,
As ever lowly Rajpoot swain,
On Mewar's still romantic plain.'

Gibraltar.

The flag that here floats proudly in the air,
The silent warders on the ramparts white,
The guns that hide in sheltered nooks from sight,
Or from the seaward scarp, their chosen lair,
Gaze on the waters with a steadfast stare,
The rock-cut embrasures ablaze at night,
The mole, the ships, the keep's commanding height,
All speak of stern resolve, and watchful care.
For leagued in arms should Europe rise once more,
To question on this steep the Lion's reign,
Swift must the deadly hail of battles pour,
As on the day when baffled France and Spain
Beheld their vaunted ships in flames ashore,
Or drifting helpless on the stormy main.

Fire Hunters.

There are no abler adepts in the art
Of woodcraft, than the gentle Gonds, who dwell
In the wild region where the mighty sal,
The hardy salei, and Briarean saj,
O'erhung with creepers of enormous bulk,
Clothe the soft uplands, and the vales that lie
Round the head-waters of the rapid Sone.

Unused to agriculture, and devoid
Of e'en such lore as is required to rear
Cattle or sheep or poultry with success,
They look alone to what their woods supply,
Gums, berries, honey, wholesome nuts and game,
To meet their wants, and thus from youth become
Experienced trappers, wary, quick of eye,
And full of rare devices to ensnare
The game that furnishes their fires with meat.

They often start at eve in knots of four,
Equipped with a slight pole of pliant wood,
From which as from a balance-beam depend
A heap of branches, and an earthen jar
With blazing fagots piled of driest wood.
This strange machine, contrived with simple art,
To cast a flaring light upon the path,
The foremost hunter on his shoulder bears,
And while the second, as he jogs, oft shakes
A rod of iron garnished with ten rings,
That jingle lightly like a bunch of keys,
The hindmost follow with their hunting poles
Of toughened cane, six yards and more in length.

When near the covert side, the jingling sound
Excites the timid hare, nay bolder game,
To scour the precincts, and detect the cause :
It tempts the open, but the occult glare
Frustrates its purpose, and it stands agaze ;
Till a quick thwack ! delivered with just aim,
Cuts short its blank surprise and life at once.

If the sport lasts an hour or two, so rich
Are all the coverts of their woods in game,
The hunters come home with a varied bag
Of hares and porcupines and spotted deer.

The Hills.

How sweet 'twere here an anchorite to dwell,
Here in the presence of this white cascade!
To muse at noon beneath this grateful shade,
With bead and crucifix to haunt this cell;
Fresh wholesome fruits to gather in the dell,
At early morn what time broad lights invade
The dew-gemmed coverts of the peaceful glade,
And listening silence broods o'er rock and fell;
With solemn cheer to mark at eve on high
The stars leap forth, to lie on this smooth stone
Strewed with crisp leaves, and hear the owlet's cry
Borne on the breeze from crag and cavern lone,
Or close in balmy sleep the languid eye,
Lulled by the deep-voiced Teesta's soothing tone.

Samarsi.

Samarsi the bold is the pride of his clan,
But he owns not an acre in broad Rajasthan;
Samarsi the bold is the hope of the true,
But his sporran is empty, his henchmen are few,
For the Moors o'er the Jumna in triumph have come,
And Samarsi the bold is an exile from home.

Though the Moslem now feasts in his hall and his bower,
And the crescent flag flutters from temple and tower,
Though the chase and the forest, the pass and the height,
Are watched by the soldiers by day and by night,
Samarsi the bold is as merry as when
His will was the law in his loved native glen.

For the roebuck still bounds by the dark haunted lake,
And the partridge still springs from the deep tangled brake,

And the perch and the salmon in silv'ry shoals gleam,
At morning and noontide in pool and in stream,
And spite of their warders on hill and on plain
Samarsi can harry his father's domain.

Though an outlaw decreed by the chiefs of the foe,
Samarsi has homage from high and from low,
For the copsewood is heavy by Saloombra park,
And the vale of Banmora at noonday is dark,
And he's ready, aye ready, right firmly to stand
By the wood or the pass with his sword in his hand.

In the cave of Pokurna, beneath the green hill,
Where the throstle keeps time to the soft-crooning rill,
Samarsi at nightfall, unknown to the Moor,
Lights his watch-fire in peace, when his labours are o'er,
And revels in freedom till morning again
Gives the signal to mount and ride down to the plain.

On an Old Romaunt.

When the night is dark and dreary, and the north wind whistles shrill,
And the snow storm drives in fury down the gorges of the hill,
Like the necromancer's mirror, when his magic perfumes burn,
Mocking Time, these curious volumes make the glorious Past return.

Fast as ripples on the river, or cloud-shadows on the grass,
As I read their quaint old pages, down my curtained chamber pass
Mitred priest, and hospitaller, armed and mounted for the fray,
Bands of bronzed condottieri, maidens fair as laughing May.

All that fancy loves to cherish, of the grand old feudal times,
Palmer guides, and weary pilgrims, wending home from distant climes,
Trembling Jews with jewel caskets, border chiefs who own no law,
Quivered bands of merry archers, mustered on the 'greene shaw.'

Norman holds, embattled belfrys, gyves, and chains, and dungeons dim,
Winding stairs, and blazing beacons, ancient arms grotesque and grim,
Pensive nuns, in quest of simples, in the lonely midnight hour,
Adepts o'er alembics chanting uncouth rhymes of mystic power.

Foreign marts, Venetian Doges, bales of precious merchandise,
Stately streets in Flemish cities, burgher crowds in peaceful guise,
Mighty dukes by guards attended, foresters in kirtles green,
Silver fonts and flaring tapers, ladies sheathed in jewels' sheen.

Moorish forts in far Grenada, portals barred and turbans blue,
Gardens green as blissful Eden, crystal fountains fair to view,
Divans in the proud Alhambra, fairy mosques of Parian stone,
Groups of Moors and whiskered Spaniards tilting round the Soldan's throne.

And enrapt I gaze in silence, like a child before a show,
Heedless in my joy and wonder, how the golden moments flow,
Till the cock's shrill ringing clarion breaks the spell and clears the air,
And I find me silent seated in my old accustomed chair.

The Terai.

The arching alders with dank moisture shone ;
Above, around, the wild vine, as I past,
Waved in slow cadence to the fever blast,
Sweeping in fitful gusts with languid moan.
The thick white mist on mouldering stem and stone,
As evening closed, a fearful shroud rolled fast ;
The blinding darkness round her mantle cast,
And quenched my hopes ere half the woods were won ;
A dip ! a rise ! clean vanished mist and shade,
And blissful Eden swam at once to sight !
Clear tops of distant hills, a smiling glade,
And modest farms, blue skies, and pastures bright,
And terraced slopes with grass and flower inlaid,
Bathed in a flood of autumn's golden light.

SHOSHEE CHUNDER DUTT,

1825–1886.

Sivajee.

AURUNGZEB'S RECEPTION OF THE MAHRATTA LEADER.

They led him to the stately hall,
  Before the royal throne,
Where, towering in the pomp of power,
  The tyrant sat alone ;
And knights and nobles stood around,
  Elate with haughty pride,
And slaves, in gorgeous tinsel dress'd,
  Awaited by their side.

He knelt before the tyrant's throne,
  But caught no courtly smile :
The monarch look'd with eye of scorn,
  Then darkly gazed awhile ;
And minions proud, whose hearts had quail'd
  When told his name of fear,
Now mock'd the valiant Sivajee
  With cold respect and sneer.

He could not bear their servile scorn—
  The scorn of vassals low,
The passions of his stubborn heart
  Were gathering on his brow ;
His bosom, plough'd with manly scars,
  The records of his fame,
Now heaved with all a warrior's wrath :
  He was not born to shame.

In dudgeon high he left the court,
  Nor ask'd the king's command ;
But found himself deceived, betray'd,
  A captive in the land.
But who can cross the fox's wile ?
  Control the eagle free ?
The royal guards are shrewd and true,
  But where is Sivajee ?

The bird has flown ; no stubborn cage
  Its wily heart could tame ;
For deadlier works of death prepare—
  He comes with sword and flame !
Ye ply to trap with subtle words ;
  That feeble art is vain ;
The trusting bird, when once deceived,
  Will never trust again.

No, ne'er again he'll cross the hall
  To cringe on servile knee,
But oft, through battle's dusky smoke,
  His blood-red sword ye'll see ;
At merry feast he may not join,
  But through the war-clouds dun,
O'er gasping chiefs and soldiers slain,
  He'll lead the carnage on.

The bravest hearts shall own with dread
  The fury of his wrath,
And sights of woe alone shall mark
  The dread avenger's path ;
With horror mute the wife shall gaze
  Upon her murder'd lord,
While yet shall glow, though wet and dim,
  The unrelenting sword.

On vengeance he will build his name,
  Till rocks aloud resound
The glory of his valiant arms,
  And quakes the unconscious ground ;
Till e'en the scorner, from his throne,
  Shall mark the kindling fire,
And wish that he had never stirr'd
  That haughty soul's dark ire.

The Warrior's Return.

When Maharajah Jeswant Singh, being defeated by Aurungzeb, fled for refuge to his own capital, his wife, with Spartan haughtiness, refused him admittance, saying "This man is an impostor, for the brave never return with dishonour. My husband sleeps on the field of battle."

Heard ye that lofty pealing sound
  Upon the balmy air,
The exulting shout that best proclaims
  The deeds which heroes dare ?

In triumph blow their trumpets proud,
  The clouds repeat their voice ;
Go, greet the laurell'd victors home,
  And bid our realms rejoice.

Let poets tune their golden harps,
  Let maidens wear their smile,
And young and old their cares lay by,
  And cease to mourn awhile.

What ! hear'st thou not their joyous din ?
  Behold, above the vale,
Their haughty plumes and ensigns red
  Are fluttering in the gale ;

And helmets cleft, and canvas torn,
  Proclaim the fighting done ;
And neighing steeds, and bloody spears,
  Announce the battle won.

Alas ! the vision mocks my sight ;
  I see no gallant throng,
No trophies meet my longing eyes ;
  Bid cease the joyous song.

That recreant slave is not my lord ;
  Ne'er thus the brave return ;
Go, bid the city-gates be barr'd,
  And leave me lone to mourn.

I know him not, I never knew
  A low, ignoble love ;
My warrior sleeps upon the moor,
  His soul hath soar'd above.

Upon the battle-field he lies,
  His garments stain'd with gore ;
With sword in hand prepared he sleeps
  To fight the battle o'er.

His shiver'd shield, his broken spear,
  Around him scatter'd lie ;
The iron-breasted Moslems shook
  To see my hero die.

Where helmets rang, where sabres smote,
  He found his gory bed ;
Join, mourners, join, and loudly raise
  The requiem of the dead.

Expel yon vile impostor hence ;
  I will not trust his tale ;
Our warriors on the crimson field
  Their chieftain's loss bewail.

The mountain-torrent rushing down
  Can ne'er its course retrace,
And souls that speed on glory's path
  Must ever onward press :

Aye, onward press—to bleed and die,
  Triumphant still in death ;
Impostor, hence ! in other lands
  Go draw thy coward breath.

Address to the Ganges.

The waves are dashing proudly down,
  Along thy sounding shore ;
Lashing, with all the storm of power,
The craggy base of mountain tower,
  Of mosque, and pagod hoar,
That darkly o'er thy waters frown ;
As if their moody spirits' sway
Could hush thy wild and boist'rous play.

Unconscious roll the surges down,
  But not unconscious thou,
Dread spirit of the roaring flood !
For ages worshipp'd as a god,
  And worshipp'd even now—
Worshipp'd and not by serf or clown ;
For sages of the mightiest fame
Have paid their homage to thy name.

Canst thou forget the glorious past,
  When, mighty as a god,
With hands and heart unfetter'd yet,
And eyes with slavish tears unwet,
  Each sable warrior trod
Thy sacred shore ; before the blast
Of Moslem conquest hurried by ;
Ere yet the Mogul spear was nigh ?

O'er crumbled thrones thy waters glide,
  Through scenes of blood and woe ;
And crown and kingdom, might and sway,
The victor's and the poet's bay,
  Ignobly sleep below.
Sole remnant of our ancient pride;
Thy waves survive the wreck of time,
And wanton free, as in their prime.

I gaze upon thy current strong
  Beneath the blaze of day ;
What conjured visions throng my sight,
Of war and carnage, death and flight !
  Thy waters to the Bay
In purple eddies sweep along,
And Freedom shrieking leaves her shrine,
Alas ! no longer now divine.

'Twas here the savage Tartar stood,
  And toss'd his brand and spear ;
The ripples of thy sacred stream
Reflected back his sabre's gleam,
  While quaked with dastard fear
The children of a haughtier blood,
No longer now a haughty race,
Their own, their sires', their land's disgrace.

But why recount our woes and shame ?
  Upon thy sacred shore
Be mine to dream of glories past,
To grieve those glories could not last,
  And muse on days of yore ;
For ever harp on former fame,
Remembering still those spirits brave
Who sleep beneath thy boist'rous wave.

Roll, Gunga, roll in all thy pride,
  Thy hallow'd groves among !
Glorious art thou in every mood,
Thou boast of India's widowhood,
  Thou theme of every song !
Blent with the murmurs of thy tide
The records of far ages lie,
And live, for thou canst never die.

The Requiem of Timour.

Sleep, perturbed spirit, sleep
  Within earth's quiet breast !
Thy task of vengeance now is o'er ;
  Rest, ruthless conqueror, rest !

As speeds the whirlwind o'er the wave
  With its resistless might,
The torrent of thy wrath has roll'd
  Upon the field of fight.

The world aghast has quaked beneath
  The terrors of thy frown ;
Thy footsteps, they have trampled o'er
  The royal neck and crown.

The burning sand, the fertile vale,
  Have groan'd beneath thy tread ;
Thy hardy legions follow'd still,
  Where thou undaunted led.

From Kabool's rock, thy crimson flag
  Stream'd proudly to the air ;
Beneath were martial shields and spears,
  And sabres red and bare.

The Indus' stormy waters fail'd
To bar the victor's path ;
And Delhi's burning towers confest
The awful Scythian's wrath.

A thousand terrors rode along
By Gunga's quaking shore ;
And hungry vultures scream'd above
Thy sacred shrine, Hurdwar.

And now he sleeps : rest, conqueror, rest !
Thy vengeful task is o'er :
The trumpet's voice, though loud it speaks,
Will wake thee never more !

The world thy triumphs mark'd with dread ;
Sleep, ruthless tyrant, sleep !
That breathless terror now has pass'd,
The world has ceased to weep.

Rest, perturbed spirit, rest !
Rest, thunder-bolt of heaven !
The avenger's rod, the victor's might,
To thee conjoint were given.

Jelaludeen Khiliji.

Malleck Feroze, otherwise called Jelaludeen, was the son of Malleck, a soldier of fortune and chief of the Afghan tribe called Khiliji. He was raised to the throne by a powerful faction, on the murder of Keikobad, of which he was believed to be the principal instigator: but he affected extreme regret at having his high office forced on him; and, while on the throne, was remarkable for his exceeding humility, clemency and simplicity of manners.

I am a king, but why forget
That I am still a man ?
And why should gilded baubles lure,
And thoughts unclean, and deeds impure
Engross life's little span ?

Who in the pride and pomp of state
Hath ever found his spirit's rest ?
In Glory's thraldom who was blest ?

What is there in a pageant's blaze
   To cheer a monarch's eye ?
And why should flattery's voice subdue,
Or why should dazzling trinkets woo,
   Or vests of purple dye,
That soul which God has deign'd to raise
Above the reach of vulgar pain,
And fortune's frown, and pride's disdain ?

I scorn the applause of servile men,
   The wicked passions shun ;
Nor would I barter for renown,
A richer jewel than my crown,
   The feelings which I own :
I seek the poor in every den ;
The rustic's cheerful hearth is mine,
I laugh with him—with him repine.

The friends with whom my footsteps ranged
   O'er barren rock and hill,
To them with haughtiness to speak,
This faithful heart would surely break,
   And be for ever still :
I find my feelings are unchanged,
Or I these royal robes would scorn,
And be again what I was born.

When I was low I ne'er repined,
   Nor cursed my humble lot ;
I never ask'd for wealth or pride,
Ne'er turn'd from poverty aside,
   My duty ne'er forgot ;

I sought for peace within my mind :
A man content I roved the green,
In folly's path was never seen.

The sick, the grieved, I tend them still
  Beside their beds of straw ;
A welcome guest where'er I come,
I always seek the poor man's home :
  My word they say is law ;
Then be fulfill'd a monarch's will,
Avaunt, fly Fear, let Discord cease,
And come and bless us meek-eyed Peace.

I ask'd not to be raised to state,
  I never sought a throne ;
With greater pleasure I could dwell,
My friends and I within a cell,
  Than thus reign all alone—
The greatest man among the great !
No, rather would I choose to be
The poorest of the company.

O Thou ! who from the lowliest life
  Hast raised me 'bove my peers,
When all the world lies hush'd in sleep,
Before Thy throne my soul doth creep,
  In penitence and tears :
Since to this state, with peril rife,
Lord ! Thou hast dragg'd me in Thy wrath,
In pity light my rugged path.

TORU DUTT.

1856–1877.

Jogadhya Uma.

"Shell-bracelets ho! Shell-bracelets ho!
  Fair maids and matrons come and buy!"
Along the road, in morning's glow,
  The pedlar raised his wonted cry.
The road ran straight, a red, red line,
  To Khirogram, for cream renowned,
Through pasture-meadows where the kine,
  In knee-deep grass, stood magic bound
And half awake, involved in mist,
  That floated in dun coils profound,
Till by the sudden sunbeams kist
  Rich rainbow hues broke all around.

"Shell-bracelets ho! Shell-bracelets ho!"
  The roadside trees still dripped with dew,
And hung their blossoms like a show.
  Who heard the cry? 'Twas but a few,
A ragged herd-boy, here and there,
  With his long stick and naked feet;
A ploughman wending to his care,
  The field from which he hopes the wheat;
An early traveller, hurrying fast
  To the next town; an urchin slow
Bound for the school; these heard and past,
  Unheeding all,—"Shell-bracelets ho!"

Pellucid spread a lake-like tank
  Beside the road now lonelier still,
High on three sides arose the bank
  Which fruit-trees shadowed at their will;

Upon the fourth side was the Ghat,
  With its broad stairs of marble white,
And at the entrance-arch there sat,
  Full face against the morning light,
A fair young woman with large eyes,
  And dark hair falling to her zone,
She heard the pedlar's cry arise,
  And eager seemed his ware to own.

" Shell-bracelets ho ! See, maiden see !
  The rich enamel sunbeam kist !
Happy, oh happy, shalt thou be,
  Let them but clasp that slender wrist ;
These bracelets are a mighty charm,
  They keep a lover ever true,
And widowhood avert, and harm,
  Buy them, and thou shalt never rue.
Just try them on ! "—She stretched her hand,
  " Oh what a nice and lovely fit !
No fairer hand, in all the land,
  And lo ! the bracelet matches it."

Dazzled the pedlar on her gazed
  Till came the shadow of a fear,
While she the bracelet arm upraised
  Against the sun to view more clear.
Oh she was lovely, but her look
  Had something of a high command
That filled with awe. Aside she shook
  Intruding curls by breezes fanned
And blown across her brows and face,
  And asked the price, which when she heard
She nodded, and with quiet grace
  For payment to her home referred.

" And where, O maiden, is thy house !
  But no, that wrist-ring has a tongue,

No maiden art thou, but a spouse,
  Happy, and rich, and fair, and young."
"Far otherwise, my lord is poor,
  And him at home thou shalt not find;
Ask for my father; at the door
  Knock loudly; he is deaf, but kind.
Seest thou that lofty gilded spire
  Above these tufts of foliage green?
That is our place; its points of fire
  Will guide thee o'er the tract between."

"That is the temple spire."—"Yes, there
  We live; my father is the priest,
The manse is near, a building fair
  But lowly to the temple's east.
When thou hast knocked, and seen him, say,
  His daughter, at Dhamaser Ghat,
Shell-bracelets bought from thee to-day,
  And he must pay so much for that.
Be sure, he will not let thee pass
  Without the value and a meal,
If he demur, or cry alas!
  No money hath he,—then reveal,

Within the small box, marked with streaks
  Of bright vermilion, by the shrine,
The key whereof has lain for weeks
  Untouched, he'll find some coin,—'tis mine.
That will enable him to pay
  The bracelet's price, now fare thee well!"
She spoke, the pedlar went away,
  Charmed with her voice, as by some spell;
While she left lonely there, prepared
  To plunge into the water pure,
And like a rose her beauty bared,
  From all observance quite secure.

Not weak she seemed, nor delicate,
  Strong was each limb of flexile grace,
All full the bust; the mien elate,
  Like her's, the goddess of the chase
On Latmos hill,—and oh, the face
  Framed in its cloud of floating hair,
No painter's hand might hope to trace
  The beauty and the glory there!
Well might the pedlar look with awe,
  For though her eyes were soft, a ray
Lit them at times, which kings who saw
  Would never dare to disobey.

On through the groves the pedlar sped
  Till full in front the sunlit spire
Arose before him. Paths which led
  To gardens trim in gay attire
Lay all around. And lo! the manse,
  Humble but neat with open door!
He paused, and blest the lucky chance
  That brought his bark to such a shore.
Huge straw ricks, log huts full of grain,
  Sleek cattle, flowers, a tinkling bell,
Spoke in a language sweet and plain,
  "Here smiling Peace and Plenty dwell."

Unconsciously he raised his cry,
  "Shell-bracelets ho!" And at his voice
Looked out the priest, with eager eye,
  And made his heart at once rejoice.
"Ho, *Sankha* pedlar! Pass not by,
  But step thou in, and share the food
Just offered on our altar high,
  If thou art in a hungry mood.

Welcome are all to this repast !
  The rich and poor, the high and low !
Come, wash thy feet, and break thy fast,
  Then on thy journey strengthened go."

"Oh thanks, good priest ! Observance due
  And greetings ! May thy name be blest !
I came on business, but I knew
  Here might be had both food and rest
Without a charge ; for all the poor
  Ten miles around thy sacred shrine
Know that thou keepest open door,
  And praise that generous hand of thine :
But let my errand first be told,
  For bracelets sold to thine this day,
So much thou owest me in gold,
  Hast thou the ready cash to pay ?

The bracelets were enamelled,—so
  The price is high."—"How ! Sold to mine ?
Who bought them, I should like to know."
  "Thy daughter, with the large black eyne,
Now bathing at the marble ghat."
  Loud laughed the priest at this reply,
"I shall not put up, friend, with that ;
  No daughter in the world have I,
An only son is all my stay ;
  Some minx has played a trick, no doubt,
But cheer up, let thy heart be gay.
  Be sure that I shall find her out."

"Nay, nay, good father, such a face
  Could not deceive, I must aver ;
At all events, she knows thy place,
  'And if my father should demur

To pay thee,'—thus she said,—' or cry
  He has no money, tell him straight
The box vermilion-streaked to try,
  That's near the shrine.' " "Well, wait,
    friend, wait!"
The priest said thoughtful and he ran
  And with the open box came back,
"Here is the price exact, my man,
  No surplus over, and no lack.

How strange! how strange! Oh blest art thou
  To have beheld her, touched her hand,
Before whom Vishnu's self must bow,
  And Brahma and his heavenly band!
Here have I worshipped her for years
  And never seen the vision bright;
Vigils and fasts and secret tears
  Have almost quenched my outward sight;
And yet that dazzling form and face
  I have not seen, and thou, dear friend,
To thee, unsought for, comes the grace,
  What may its purport be, and end?

How strange! How strange! Oh happy thou!
  And couldst thou ask no other boon
Than thy poor bracelet's price? That brow
  Resplendent as the autumn moon
Must have bewildered thee, I trow,
  And made thee lose thy senses all."
A dim light on the pedlar now
  Began to dawn; and he let fall
His bracelet basket in his haste,
  And backward ran the way he came;
What meant the vision fair and chaste,
  Whose eyes were they,—those eyes of flame?

Swift ran the pedlar as a hind,
The old priest followed on his trace,
They reached the Ghat but could not find
The lady of the noble face.
The birds were silent in the wood,
The lotus flowers exhaled a smell
Faint, over all the solitude,
A heron as a sentinel
Stood by the bank. They called,—in vain,
No answer came from hill or fell,
The landscape lay in slumber's chain,
E'en Echo slept within her cell.

Broad sunshine, yet a hush profound!
They turned with saddened hearts to go;
Then from afar there came a sound
Of silver bells;—the priest said low,
"O Mother, Mother, deign to hear,
The worship-hour has rung; we wait
In meek humility and fear.
Must we return home desolate?
Oh come, as late thou cam'st unsought,
Or was it but an idle dream?
Give us some sign if it was not,
A word, a breath, or passing gleam."

Sudden from out the water sprung
A rounded arm, on which they saw
As high the lotus buds among
It rose, the bracelet white, with awe.
Then a wide ripple tost and swung
The blossoms on that liquid plain,
And lo! the arm so fair and young
Sank in the waters down again.

They bowed before the mystic Power,
And as they home returned in thought,
Each took from thence a lotus flower
In memory of the day and spot.

Years, centuries, have passed away,
And still before the temple shrine
Descendants of the pedlar pay
Shell bracelets of the old design
As annual tribute. Much they own
In land and gold,—but they confess
From that eventful day alone
Dawned on their industry,—success.
Absurd may be the tale I tell,
Ill-suited to the marching times ;
I loved the lips from which it fell,
So let it stand among my rhymes.

The Lotus.

Love came to Flora asking for a flower
That would of flowers be undisputed queen,
The lily and the rose, long, long had been
Rivals for that high honour. Bards of power
Had sung their claims. " The rose can never tower
Like the pale lily with her Juno mien "—
" But is the lily lovelier ? " Thus between
Flower factions rang the strife in Psyche's bower.
Give me a flower delicious as the rose
And stately as the lily in her pride "—
" But of what colour ? "—" Rose-red," Love first chose,
Then prayed,—" No, lily-white,—or, both provide ; "
And Flora gave the lotus, " rose-red " dyed,
And " lily-white,"—the queenliest flower that blows.

Our Casuarina Tree.

Like a huge Python, winding round and round,
The rugged trunk, indented deep with scars,
Up to its very summit near the stars,
A creeper climbs, in whose embraces bound
No other tree could live. But gallantly
The giant wears the scarf, and flowers are hung
In crimson clusters all the boughs among,
Whereon all day are gathered bird and bee;
And oft at nights the garden overflows
With one sweet song that seems to have no close,
Sung darkling from our tree, while men repose.

When first my casement is wide open thrown
At dawn, my eyes delighted on it rest;
Sometimes, and most in winter,—on its crest
A grey baboon sits statue-like alone
Watching the sunrise; while on lower boughs
His puny offspring leap about and play;
And far and near kokilas hail the day;
And to their pastures wend our sleepy cows;
And in the shadow, on the broad tank cast
By that hoar tree, so beautiful and vast,
The water-lilies spring, like snow enmassed.

But not because of its magnificence
Dear is the Casuarina to my soul;
Beneath it we have played; though years may roll,
O sweet companions, loved with love intense,
For your sakes, shall the tree be ever dear!
Blent with your images, it shall arise
In memory, till the hot tears blind mine eyes!
What is that dirge-like murmur that I hear
Like the sea breaking on a shingle-beach?
It is the tree's lament, an eerie speech,
That haply to the unknown land may reach.

Unknown, yet well-known to the eye of faith !
  Ah, I have heard that wail far, far away
  In distant lands, by many a sheltered bay,
When slumbered in his cave the water-wraith,
  And the waves gently kissed the classic shore
Of France or Italy, beneath the moon,
When earth lay tranced in a dreamless swoon :—
  And every time the music rose, before
Mine inner vision rose a form sublime,—
Thy form, O Tree, as in my happy prime
I saw thee, in my own loved native clime.

Therefore I fain would consecrate a lay
  Unto thy honour, Tree, beloved of those
  Who now in blessed sleep, for aye, repose,
Dearer than life to me, alas ! were they !
  Mayst thou be numbered when my days are done
With deathless trees—like those in Borrowdale,
Under whose awful branches lingered pale
  "Fear, trembling Hope, and Death, the skeleton,
And Time the shadow ; " and though weak the verse
That would thy beauty fain, oh fain rehearse,
  May Love defend thee from Oblivion's curse !

Morning Serenade.*

From Victor Hugo.

Still barred thy doors !—The far east glows,
  The morning wind blows fresh and free,
Should not the hour that wakes the rose
    Awaken also thee ?

* This poem, quoted in the preface of "Ancient Ballads and Legends of Hindustan" as the work of Toru Dutt, has been assigned rightly to her elder sister, Aru Dutt, some of whose translations appear in "A Sheaf Gleaned in French Fields."

No longer sleep,
Oh, listen now !
I wait and weep,
But where art thou ?

All look for thee, Love, Light and Song ;
Light, in the sky deep red above,
Song, in the lark of pinion strong,
And in my heart, true Love.
No longer sleep,
Oh, listen now !
I wait and weep,
But where art thou ?

Apart we miss our nature's goal,
Why strive to cheat our destinies ?
Was not my love made for thy soul ?
Thy beauty for mine eyes ?
No longer sleep,
Oh, listen now !
I wait and weep,
But where art thou ?

ROMESH CHANDER DUTT,
1848–1909.

The Legend of Balaki.

Balaki, a learned Brahman,
Proud of knowledge, proud of lore,
Versed he was in many a sastra,
Travelled many a distant shore,
In the land of Usinara,
And in Matsya he had been,
Panchala and the Kuru kingdoms,
Videha and the Kasi seen.

Ajatasatru, learned monarch,
Ruled in Kasi's mighty land,
Unto him repaired the Brahman,
In his palace rich and grand.
" Blessed be thy rule, O monarch !
O'er this kingdom rich and broad,
I will speak to thee of Brahman,
I will speak to thee of God ! "

" Welcome, welcome, learned priest ! "
Ajatasatru thus replied,—
" For thy holy speech accept
A thousand kine of finest breed !
Every learned Brahman hies
To Janaka, holy king,—
Welcome thou to Kasi's court,
And a Brahman's blessings bring ! "

" List then, king ! to words of wisdom,"—
    Proud Balaki thus began,—
" Knowest thou the radiant Soul
    Dwelleth in the radiant sun ?
  Him I worship ! "—said Balaki.
    " Not so ! "—answered thus the king,
" For the sun is mighty, glorious,
    But is a created thing ! "

" Knowest thou the lunar crescent,
    Shining in the starry sky ?
  Knowest thou the beauteous Soul,
    Dwelleth there serene and high ?
  Him I worship ! "—said Balaki.
    " Not so ! "—answered thus the king,
" For the moon is bright and beauteous
    But is a created thing ! "

" Dost thou know the forked lightning,
    Flashing through the lurid sky ?
  Dost thou know the dreaded Soul,
    Dwelleth there, terrific, high ?
  Him I worship ! "—said Balaki.
    " Not so "—answered thus the king,
" For the lightning is terrific,
    But is a created thing ! "

" Dost thou know the deep-voiced thunder,
    Pealing through the echoing sky ?
  Dost thou know the soul that dwelleth
    In that sound, terrific, high ?
  Him I worship ! "—said Balaki.
    " Not so ! "—answered thus the king ;
" For the thunder is terrific,
    But is a created thing ! "

Long he toiled, the learned Brahman,
  Power Almighty to explain,
Quoted he from holy sastras,
  Argued long, but argued vain !
To his reasons, to his learning,
  Ever answered thus the king,
" Mighty wondrous is all nature,
  But it is created thing ! "

Still he toiled, the learned Brahman,
  To explain the God on high,
Spoke of fire and spoke of ether,
  Spoke of water and of sky,
Spoke of shadow and reflection,
  Spoke of echo and of sound,
Argued about dreams and slumber,
  But solution none he found !

Silently the boastful Brahman
  Bent his head in grief and shame,
Sad he was, the learned Brahman,
  To a wiser king he came !
" Thus far,"—said the monarch gently,
  " Thus far doth thy wisdom go ! "
" Thus far ! wise and learned monarch !
  Teach me what you further know ! "

With the fuel, meek and humble,
  Balaki as student came,
Seeking knowledge from the monarch,
  Great in learning as in fame.
" He who made the sun and moon,
  And the sky and earth so broad,
He who breathed all Nature forth,—
  He is Brahman, He is God ! "

Mahabharata.

GANDHARI'S LAMENT FOR THE SLAIN.

Stainless Queen and stainless woman, ever righteous ever good,
Stately in her mighty sorrow on the field Gandhari stood!
Strewn with skulls and clotted tresses, darkened by the stream of gore,
With the limbs of countless warriors was the red field covered o'er,
Elephants and steeds of battle, car-borne chiefs untimely slain,
Headless trunks and heads dissevered filled the red and ghastly plain!
And the long-drawn howl of jackals o'er the scene of carnage rings,
And the vulture and the raven flap their dark and loathsome wings,
Feasting on the blood of warriors foul *pisachas* fill the air,
Viewless forms of hungry *rakshas* limb from limb the corpses tear!
Through this scene of death and carnage was the ancient monarch led,
Kuru dames with faltering footsteps stepped amidst the countless dead,
And a piercing wail of anguish burst upon the echoing plain,
As they saw their sons or fathers, brothers, lords, amidst the slain,
As they saw wolves of the jungle feed upon the destined prey,
Darksome wanderers of the midnight prowling in the light of day!
Shriek of pain and wail of anguish o'er the ghastly field resound,
And their feeble footsteps falter and they sink upon the ground,

Sense and life desert the mourners as they faint in common grief,
Death-like swoon succeeding sorrow yields the sufferers short relief !
Then a mighty sigh of anguish from Gandhari's bosom broke,
Gazing on her anguished daughters unto Krishna thus she spoke :
" Mark my unconsoled daughters, widowed queens of Kuru's house,
Wailing for their dear departed, like the osprey for her spouse !
How each cold and fading feature wakes in them a woman's love,
How amidst the lifeless warriors still with restless steps they rove,
Mothers hug their slaughtered children all unconscious in their sleep,
Widows bend upon their husbands and in ceaseless sorrow weep !
Mighty Bhishma, hath he fallen ? quenched is archer Karna's pride ?
Drupad monarch of Panchala sleeps by foeman Drona's side ?
Shining mail and costly jewels, royal bangles strew the plain,
Golden garlands rich and burnished deck the chiefs untimely slain,
Lances hurled by stalwart fighters, clubs of mighty wrestlers killed,
Swords and bows of ample measure, quivers still with arrows filled !
Mark the unforgotten heroes, jungle prowlers 'mid them stray,
On their brow and mailed bosoms heedless perch the birds of prey !
Mark the great unconquered heroes famed on earth from west to east,
Kankas perch upon their foreheads, hungry wolves upon them feast !

Mark the kings, on softest cushion scarce the needed rest they found,
How they lie in peaceful slumber on the hard and reddened ground!
Mark the youths who morn and evening listed to the minstrel's song,
In their ear the loathsome jackal doth his doleful wail prolong!
Mark the chieftains with their maces and the swords of trusty steel,
Still they grasp their well tried weapons,—do they still the life-pulse feel?"

FUNERAL RITES.

Victor of a deathful battle, sad Yudhishthir viewed the plain,
Friends and kinsmen, kings and chieftains, countless troops untimely slain,
And he spake to wise Sudharman, pious priest of Kuru's race,
Unto Sanjay, unto Dhaumya, to Vidura full of grace,
Spake unto the brave Yujutsu, Kuru's last surviving chief,
Spake to faithful Indrasena and to warriors sunk in grief;
"Pious rites are due to foemen and to friends and kinsmen slain,
None shall lack a fitting funeral, none shall perish on the plain."
Wise Vidura and his comrades sped on sacred duty bound,
Sandalwood and scented aloes, oil and *ghee* and perfumes found,
Silken robes of costly splendour, fabrics by the artist wove,
Dry wood from the thorny jungle, perfume from the scented grove,
Shattered cane and splintered lances, hewed and ready for the fire,
Piled and ranged in perfect order into many a funeral pyre.
Kings and princes, noble warriors, were in rank and order laid,
And with streams of melted butter were the rich libations made,

Blazed the fire with wondrous radiance by the rich libations fed,
Sanctifying and consuming mortal remnants of the dead.
Brave Duryodhan and his brothers, Salya of the mighty car,
Bhurisravas king of nations, Jayadratha famed in war,
Abhimanyu son of Arjun, Lakshman proud Duryodhan's son,
Somadatta and the Srinjays famed for deeds of valour done,
Matsya's monarch proud Virata, Drupad fair Panchala's king,
And his sons, Panchala's princes, whose great deeds the minstrels sing,
Cultured monarch of Kosala and Gandhara's wily lord,
Karna proud and peerless archer, matchless with his flaming sword,
Bhagadatta eastern monarch, all resistless in his car,
Ghatotkacha son of Bhima, Alambusha famed in war,
And a hundred other monarchs all received the pious rite,
Till the radiance of the fire-light chased the shadows of the night!
Pitri-medha, due to fathers, was performed with pious care,
Hymns and wails and lamentations mingled in the midnight air,
Sacred songs of *rik* and *saman* rose amidst the women's wail,
And the creatures of the wide earth heard the sound subdued and pale!
Smokeless and with radiant lustre shone each red and lighted pyre,
Like the planets of the bright sky throbbing with celestial fire!
Countless myriads, nameless, friendless, from each court and camp afar,
From the east and west collected, fell in Kuru-Kshetra's war,
Thousand fires for them were lighted, they received the pious rite,
Such was good Yudhishthir's mandate, such was wise Vidura's might,
All the dead were burned to ashes, and the sacred rite was o'er,
Dhrita-rashtra and Yudhishthir slowly walked to Ganga's shore.

NARENDRA NATH DUTTA (Swami Vivekananda),
1862–1902.

The Cup.

This is your cup—the cup assigned to you
From the beginning. Nay, My child, I know
How much of that dark drink is your own brew
Of fault and passion, ages long ago,
In the deep years of yesterday, I knew.

This is your road—a painful road and drear.
I made the stones that never give you rest.
I set your friend in pleasant ways and clear,
And he shall come, like you, unto My breast.
But you, My child, must travel here.

This is your task. It has no joy nor grace,
But 'tis not meant for any other hand,
And in My universe hath measured place,
Take it. I do not bid you understand.
I bid you close your eyes to see MY face.

ROBY DUTT,

1883–1918.

On Tibet.

Deep in the bosom dark of mystery,
Housed in the gleam of days that are no more
And dreams that like her Himalayas soar
To height incredible—methinks I see
The land of mystic faith and lamas hoar !

A glamour thro' the creeping sunset steals,
Weird Tibet, o'er thy snow-encircled brow ;
A glamour from the Occident, that now,
Silent, pursues thy gloom-engirdled heels,
Mother of fossil modes and customs thou !

Thou mighty miracle of centuries,
To us, the dwellers in the setting sun,
Perpetual dream-land, child of sunrise dun,
Who "teasest out of thought" man's memories,
Grim in thy glory, till thy race be run !

Land of the faith by pensive Buddha rear'd,
Where thought is stable, prayers are roll'd by wheels,
Faith moves with a dull motion as she feels
Her way thro' gloom of births, where Fate is fear'd,
God is unknown, and man in darkness reels !

To Britain.

To Britain, Queen of all the Seas,
Whose Alfred first did show her might,
Whose Nelson, strong and bold of sprite,
Did waft her fame from breeze to breeze.

The land where Caedmon saw the light,
Where Chaucer shaped his harmonies,
Whose Shakespeare fathom'd all that is,
Whose Milton rose to starry height.

To her whose light shall e'er increase,
Whose might in countless foemen's spite
From land to land shall spread aright,
Whose right to rule shall ne'er decrease,

To her who ever shall be bright,
I, prone to perish, offer these
Decaying, dying melodies,
I, rushing into endless night.

Sir Asutosh Mookerjee.

He rose, a meteor, in the midst of men
To awe the world with splendour : many a star,
That might in other skies have shone afar,
Beside him paled, and swam not into ken.

His lore with glory fill'd the quarters then,
And won him such a name as nought could mar :
He fought, and gain'd success without a scar,
A valiant knight, whose weapon was his pen.

Good-temper'd, even-minded, patient, wise,
He lent his aid wherever he could meet
A man of promise that deserved to rise :

In dealing justice fairly, none could beat
His breadth of view, and none the solemn guise
In which all fine distinctions he would greet.

Indians at the Front.

Fight for the cause of Britain and of right,
Ye Indians brave, and lay the tyrant low,
A 'cultured' yet at heart a savage foe,
That dares astound the world with ruthless might.

For peace, for commerce and for freedom fight,
Fight to relieve a hapless nation's woe,
That in the cause of all the world did throw
Her lot in with your king in terror's spite.

Your country needs no tyrant's lip-deep lore
Her old enlightenment to vindicate,
That placed her high among the states of yore :

For valour India always has been great,
And ye are India's sons, and—what is more—
Fit partners of a world-embracing State.

PROFULLA RANJAN DAS.

1881–

Refusal.

Ah, not to-night !—for thrilled yet wild with fire,
The night would whisper burning words to me,
And I should blindly search Eternity
For passion fit to crown the wild desire
To-night gives birth to !—and that passion's hire
Summoned from all the times would ever be
A bitter shame and joyless memory,
—A thing whereon would tremble Heaven's just ire !

For I would love thee only with my soul,
And build thereby a palace strong, secure,
To stand amidst the vain pomps that allure
And leave but corpses as they onward roll !
Oh, then, at last when Death demands its toll,
There's something to remember,—calm and pure !

The Quest.

I stepped into the dusty thoroughfare,
Where men with weary footsteps trod the earth,
And sought the secrets of their death and birth
In heat and passion of the noon-day air !
—In life that has been lived in black despair,
Or in the splendour of the city's worth,
Where mortals moving with no joy or mirth
Have yet aspired to do, conceive, and dare !

And one above them all cried out to me,
" Alas, alas,—I gave a life's devotion,
To drag the secrets of Eternity

From objects whirling with the earth's swift motion,
And now I think I'll wander never more,
What, if those secrets waited at my door ? "

Youth and Age.

Do you remember, how one night,
When never rose a star on high,
We stepped into the dubious light
Beneath the silence of the sky,
—You wondered,—so did I !

Your life was of the sun and flower,
But mine was of the autumn leaf,
And we imagined every hour
Would take us farther from our grief,
Forgetting time, the thief !

And yet the thief was on the wing,
And caught me gray—but you, pure white !
And now because life's splendours cling
Unto the freshness of your light,
I wonder, was I right ?

A Lament.

Alas, alas !—the roses cried despairing,
That leaf by leaf our glory should decay !
That all our splendours should be earth and clay,
And dream-like fade for all our crimson daring !
No more the winds our raptures wide are bearing,
—No more our fragrance doth uplift the day,
And passionate pilgrims now no more do stray,
Around us dreamless, death's dark splendours wearing !

Yet shall we sigh and raise the mournful wail,
Because our Beauty now has ceased to be !
Nay, tho' to-day our youth and glory pale,
What is to-day to all Eternity !
For in fresh raptures of this radiant earth
Dead roses come again to crimson birth !

SARJOINI NAIDU.

1879–

The Pardah Nashin.

Her life is a revolving dream
Of languid and sequestered ease ;
Her girdles and her fillets gleam
Like changing fires on sunset seas ;
Her raiment is like morning mist,
Shot opal, gold and amethyst.

From thieving light of eyes impure,
From coveting sun or wind's caress,
Her days are guarded and secure
Behind her carven lattices,
Like jewels in a turbaned crest,
Like secrets in a lover's breast.

But though no hand unsanctioned dares
Unveil the mysteries of her grace,
Time lifts the curtain unawares,
And Sorrow looks into her face—
Who shall prevent the subtle years,
Or shield a woman's eyes from tears ?

To a Buddha Seated on a Lotus.

Lord Buddha, on thy Lotus-throne,
With praying eyes and hands elate,
What mystic rapture dost thou own,
Immutable and ultimate ?
What peace, unravished of our ken,
Annihilate from the world of men ?

The wind of change for ever blows
Across the tumult of our way,
To-morrow's unborn griefs depose
The sorrows of our yesterday.
Dream yields to dream, strife follows strife,
And Death unweaves the webs of Life.

For us the travail and the heat,
The broken secrets of our pride,
The strenuous lessons of defeat,
The flower deferred, the fruit denied ;
But not the peace, supremely won,
Lord Buddha, of thy Lotus-throne.

With futile hands we seek to gain
Our inaccessible desire,
Diviner summits to attain,
With faith that sinks and feet that tire ;
But nought shall conquer or control
The heavenward hunger of our soul.

The end, elusive and afar,
Still lures us with its beckoning flight,
And all our mortal moments are
A session of the Infinite.
How shall we reach the great, unknown
Nirvana of thy Lotus-throne ?

The Gift of India.

Is there aught you need that my hands withhold,
Rich gifts of raiment or grain or gold ?
Lo ! I have flung to the East and West,
Priceless treasures torn from my breast,
And yielded the sons of my stricken womb
To the drum-beats of duty, the sabres of doom.

Gathered like pearls in their alien graves
Silent they sleep by the Persian waves,
Scattered like shells on Egyptian sands,
They lie with pale brows and brave, broken hands,
They are strewn like blossoms mown down by chance
On the blood-brown meadows of Flanders and France.

Can ye measure the grief of the tears I weep
Or compass the woe of the watch I keep?
Or the pride that thrills thro' my heart's despair,
And the hope that comforts the anguish of prayer?
And the far sad glorious vision I see
Of the torn red banners of Victory?

When the terror and tumult of hate shall cease,
And life be refashioned on anvils of peace,
And your love shall offer memorial thanks
To the comrades who fought in your dauntless ranks,
And you honour the deeds of the deathless ones,
Remember the blood of my martyred sons!

Suttee.

Lamp of my life, the lips of Death
Have blown thee out with their sudden breath;
Naught shall revive thy vanished spark—
Love, must I dwell in the living dark?

Tree of my life, Death's cruel foot
Hath crushed thee down to thy hidden root;
Nought shall restore thy glory fled—
Shall the blossom live when the tree is dead?

Life of my life, Death's bitter sword
Hath severed us like a broken word,
Rent us in twain who are but one—
Shall the flesh survive when the soul is gone?

A Challenge to Fate.

Why will you vex me with your futile conflict,
Why will you strive with me, O foolish Fate?
You cannot break me with your poignant envy,
You cannot slay me with your subtle hate:
For all the cruel folly you pursue
I will not cry with suppliant hands to you.

You may perchance wreck in your bitter malice
The radiant empire of mine eager eyes—
Say, can you rob my memory's dear dominion
O'er sunlit mountains and sidereal skies?
In my enduring treasuries I hold
Their ageless splendour of unravished gold.

You may usurp the kingdoms of my hearing—
Say, shall my scatheless spirit cease to hear
The bridal rapture of the blowing valleys,
The lyric pageant of the passing year,
The sounding odes and singing harmonies
Of battling tempests and unconquered seas?

Yea, you may smite my mouth to throbbing silence,
Pluck from my lips power of articulate words—
Say, shall my heart lack its familiar language
While earth has nests for her mellifluous birds?
Shall my impassioned heart forget to sing
With the ten thousand voices of the spring?

Yea, you may quell my blood with sudden anguish,
Fetter my limbs with some compelling pain—
How will you daunt my free, far-journeying fancy
That rides upon the pinions of the rain?
How will you tether my triumphant mind,
Rival and fearless comrade of the wind?

Tho' you deny the hope of all my being,
Betray my love, my sweetest dream destroy,
Yet will I slake my individual sorrow
At the deep source of Universal joy—
O Fate, in vain you hanker to control
My frail, serene, indomitable soul.

MANMOHAN GHOSE,
1869–

A Song of Britannia.

1

Muse, who art quick to fire
At the least noble thing,
And frankest praise to bring
Upon the quivering lyre,
Why art thou slow to sing
Now when the world beclouds
With battle, such as shrouds
Earth in a mist of tears?
For want of heart belike,
While thunder sings afar
And even the bravest fears.
Seek'st thou a theme for song
No fears can ever wrong,
No tears can tarnish? Strike
And sing Britannia.

2

Britannia the fair,
Whom oceans girdle round,
With hill and valley crowned,
And purest wash of air
From her Atlantic bound.
What heaths so fresh as hers
With blossom? and how stirs
The soft wind in her pines.
Earth's fairest isle, 'tis said,
Where all things lovely are.

Yet beauty there not mines
Strength ; for no cliff is there
No headland calmly fair
But fringed with wild sprays wed
To shout Britannia.

3

Britannia the strong,
Whom God designed should queen
The Ocean plain, serene
Though threat'ning foes bethrong :
Whose fate shall not belong,
While round her, every deck
Bristling with cannon, speck
The seas her angry fleet.
Not earth to dominate
Or to embroil with war
Tower they : 'tis to keep sweet
The world's dear peace they bulk
So with their silent hulk
In all eyes power, elate
To speak Britannia.

4

Britannia the free,
Of soil so virtuous, such
No foot of slave can touch
But walks at liberty.
The staff she is, the crutch
By whom weak lands arise,
Who nourished in her eyes
Grow, and shake off the sloth
Of old anarchic power.
Two richly tokens are
Of her boon influence, both :
What man of Ind or Nile
Who sees his fat fields smile

But his lips burst aflower
To praise Britannia.

5

Britannia the sage,
With her own history wise ;
The stars were her allies
To write that ample page.
'Twas her victorious eyes
The vantage saw, whence she
To this wide regency
Through acts adventurous won :
Which if from strife and jar
She keep, the secret learn
From her mild brow alone ;
How, not the world to daunt
Or power imperial flaunt
She makes the queen'd earth yearn
To serve Britannia.

6

Britannia the good,
With her own heart at school,
Whom flatterer cannot fool
Nor rebel sour ; at flood
Her own strength taught to rule.
Hers are the mighty hands
That o'er a hundred lands
Weave good from dawn to gray.
Like fond words from afar
Hers are the winged sails
O'er ocean : words are they
Which in a moment bring
Her brood beneath her wing ;
And none so small that fails
To knit Britannia.

7

Britannia wide-flung
  Over the globe ; its half
  Her children, whether graff
Or scion mother-sprung ;
  Sons, now to be her staff
When her path glooms ; though Rhine,
Danube and Elbe combine
  Of these (O idlest dream !),
To reave her. Hers they are,
  Rous'd, ardent in her right !
From Ganges utmost stream
  Far as Canadian firs
  And bush Australian, hers,
Joined even in hell's despite
  To help Britannia.

8

Britannia the heart
  And brain that bulwarks power ;
  See, at the crucial hour
How well she bears her part !
  From fields how peaceful flower
In millions arms and men !
Which now she pours again
  To those old battlefields,
France, Flanders ; makes her star
  Of glory that she shields
The weak, confronts the strong.
  Brute force let others sing ;
  She shows in everything
To her it shall belong
  To be—Britannia.

9

Britannia, sublime
  To flame in generous deed ;
  In others' cause to bleed.
So to the end of time
  It shall be. Once she freed
The Iberian. Wellington
And Torres Vedras spun
  The lines of victory then.
Another Trafalgar
  The bleak North Seas await ;
Where her fleet towers the main ;
  Each mighty battleship
  Charged to the very lip
With thunder. Big with fate
  They loom Britannia.

To Sir Jagadish Chandra Bose.

(*Translated from a poem by Sir Rabindranath Tagore.*)

Young image of what old *Rishi* of Ind
Art thou, O Arya savant, Jagadish ?
What unseen hermitage hast thou raised up
From 'neath the dry dust of this city of stone ?
Amidst the crowd's mad turmoil, whence hast thou
That peace in which thou in an instant stoodst
Alone at the deep centre of all things—
Where dwells the One alone in sun, moon, flowers,
In leaves, and beasts and birds, and dust and stones,
—Where still one sleepless Life on its own lap
Rocks all things with a wordless melody,
All things that move or that seem motionless !
While we were drunk with the remote and vain
Dead glories of our past,—in alien dress
Walking and talking in an alien tongue,

In the caricature of other men—
Their style, their bearing,—while we shouted, yell'd
Frog-like with swollen throat in our dark well,
O, in what vast remoteness wert thou then ?
Where didst thou spread thy hush'd and lonely mat—
Thy mat of meditation ? Thou, thy mind
Curdling into calm gravity, didst plunge
In thy great quest after the viewless ray,
Beyond the utmost borders of this world
Of visible form, there where the *Rishis* old
Oped, and passed in beyond the lion-gates
Of the Manifold and stood before the One,
Silent in awe and wonder, with joined hands !
O Hermit, call thou in the authentic words
Of that old hymn called Sama ; "Rise ! Awake !"
Call to the man who boasts his *Sastric* lore
From vain pedantic wranglings profitless,
Call to that foolish braggart to come forth
Out on the face of Nature, this broad earth.
Send forth this call unto thy scholar band ;
Together round thy sacrifice of fire
Let them all gather. So may our India,
Our ancient land, unto herself return.
O once again return to steadfast work,
To duty and devotion, to her trance
Of earnest meditation ; let her sit
Once more unruffled, greedless, strifeless, pure
O once again upon her lofty seat
And platform, teacher of all other lands.

London.

Farewell, sweetest country ; out of my heart, you roses,
Wayside roses, nodding the slow traveller to keep.
Too long have I drowsed alone in the meadows deep,
Too long alone endured the silence Nature espouses.

O, the rush, the rapture of life !—throngs, lights, houses !
This is London. I wake as a sentinel from sleep.

Stunned with the fresh thunder, the harsh delightful noises,
I move entranced on the thronging pavement. How sweet,
To eyes sated with green, the dusty brick-walled street !
And the lone spirit, of self so weary, how it rejoices
To be lost in others, bathed in the tones of human voices,
And feel hurried along the happy tread of feet.

And a sense of vast sympathy my heart almost crazes,
The warmth of kindred hearts in thousands beating with mine.
Each fresh face, each figure, my spirit drinks like wine,
Thousands endlessly passing. Violets, daisies,
What is your charm to the passionate charm of faces,
This ravishing reality, this earthliness divine ?

O murmur of men more sweet than all the wood's caresses.
How sweet only to be an unknown leaf that sings
In the forest of life ! Cease, nature, thy whisperings,
Can I talk with leaves, or fall in love with breezes ?
Beautiful boughs, your shade not a human pang appeases,
This is London. I lie, and twine in the roots of things.

Baby.

Baby dear ! and shall we sever ?
All your own
Mother is, and yours alone.
Father goes, he cares not he !
Comes, and now from other shores,
Baby dear, your deity
Woos he, and adores.
Never heed him ! he was never
Yours !

My one bliss, and would you lonely
Leave my heart,
Thus from mother's lap to part?
O what is it, charm of charms,
Seek your lips incarnadine,
Stretching forth your little arms,
With that cry divine?
Enchantment! art thou not only
Mine?

Fret not so, nor fear my raiment:
Heed not thou!
Softly though he flatters now.
Woods nor whispers thinks she sweet,
Mother, to thy vague murmurs:
Men, the world, the roaring street,
Father, he prefers.
Hers you are 'gainst every claimant,
Hers!

Leave him! Not a kiss deserves he
Lonely here
To forsake us, baby dear.
Toils and troubles all the week
They possess him, toils like tares
For the rose of baby's cheek
Not a thought he cares.
'Tis for them his heart preserves he,
Theirs!

Laughing, see, has baby known him,
And small hands
Stretching out, his beard demands.
O his flattery well I know,
Sweet he comes, as April showers;

Wait, poor prattler, he will go,
False as April flowers.
No, my joy, we cannot own him
Ours.

From his arms to keep you? Never!
Baby dear!
From his arms, your native sphere.
Home from labour comes he tired,
You and I, his only bliss.
Crown him, crown our king desired
To adore and kiss,
You and I his slaves forever,
His.

Poplar, Beech, and Weeping Willow.

Shapely poplar shivering white, poplar like a maiden,
Thinking, musing softly here so light and so unladen
That with every breath and stir perpetually you gladden,
Teach me your still secrecy of thoughts that never sadden.

From the heavy-hearted earth, earth of grief and passion,
Maiden, would you spring with me, and leave men's lowly fashion?
Skyward lift with me your thoughts in cumberless elation,
Every leaf and every shoot a virgin aspiration.

The blue day, the floating clouds, the stars shall you for palace
Proffer their pure world of pomp, dawn her rosy chalice,
Where the birds are you shall wing and revel to be lonely,
In the clear of heaven to spire and sway with breezes only.

Beech of lofty aisles the queen, beech of trees the lady,
Soaring to a tower of sighs in branches soft and shady,

You that sunward lift your strength to make of shadow duty,
Teach me tree your heavenly height and earth-remembering beauty.

Maiden, would you soar like me with sky-upclouding tresses ?
Beauty into bounty change, bend down the eye that blesses,
Make from heaven a shelter cool for shepherd and sheep silly,
Shadow with shadiness hot rose and fainting lily.

Through your glorious heart of gloom the noonday wind awaking
In an ecstasy shall set swaying, blowing, shaking
Leafy branches, in their nests set the sweet birds rocking,
Till their happy song breaks out the noonday ardour mocking.

Willow sweet, willow sad, willow by the river
Taught by pensive love to droop where ceaseless waters shiver,
Teach me steadfast sorrower your mournful grace of graces
Weeping to make beautiful the silent water places.

Maiden, would you learn of me the loveliness of mourning,
Weep into the chill wan wave strength, hardness, lofty scorning ;
Drench your drooping soul in tears content to love and languish,
Gaze in sorrow's looking-glass and see the face of anguish.

In the very wash of woe as your bowed soul shall linger,
You shall touch the sheer bright stars and on the moon set finger.
You shall hear where brooks have birth the mountain pines' emotion
Catch upon the broadening stream the sound and swell of ocean.

Myvanwy.

Virgin darkness, wet and deep
Where dwells but April, dwells but sleep,
What presence clear
Like a beam has entered here ?
What lov'd footstep, that the trees
Freshen their soliloquies,
Birds break into louder lays ?
All fair Nature's heart runs wild
To remember her sweet child :
In the wood Myvanwy strays !

O what gladness thrills her through
Her wayward darling back to woo
From life again,
Thought, and passion, stir and men !
Clasp her now ! From that great lure
O sweet Nature, clasp her sure,
Where no alien eye perceives !
Lead her where dim brooks have birth,
Fill her with the smell of earth,
Shut her in a thousand leaves.

Born in foliage like the flowers,
Myvanwy, to that world of ours
Of throng and street
O how strayed your vernal feet ?
There where not a daisy smiles,
There where green earth's pale exiles
Toil and toil and never cease !
"Who is this ?" the passer said :
Rustic grass was in your tread,
In your laughter the wild breeze !

Ah ! no gift of heath to city ;
It was love led you, love and pity
To my sad heart,
Child, your rapture to impart.
The fast-bound, like wintry earth,
Your intoxicating mirth
Loosed and rained delightful showers :
Showed me where their song birds borrow,
All the uselessness of sorrow,
All the joy of April flowers !

The Garden Passion.

It is a garden, shy and sweet,
For youth and tongue-tied passion meet ;
A green dim garden shaded deep,
Breathing of lilies, love, and sleep.
Here only flowers in darkness grow ;
Here only whispering waters flow,
And fishes glide, and linnets sing,
And Summer dances with the Spring,
And here in evenings gradual gloom
Have Julian and Irene come.

Speechless they stand beneath the shade
The burning youth, the lovely maid.
Bashfully droop'd the lashes sheathe
The splendour of her eyes beneath ;
And o'er her cheek and brow of snow
The virgin roses come and go.
His heart too strong, his tongue too weak,
Only his lustrous eyes can speak ;
And they seem all one pent desire
An incommunicable fire !

Conscious of that impassioned gaze
She turns away her glowing face

As though too rich a joy and shame
In that deep crimson mantling came.
And with averted cheek and hands
Folded one rapturous moment stands.
Empresslike she smiles, and fain
Would linger o'er his gorgeous pain.
But ah ! that passion-eaten look
Her gentle bosom cannot brook.
Tears start into her eyes : she turns
With shining eyes, and cheek that burns.
Love and reluctant maidenhood
Her heart impelled, her heart withstood,
A rosy strife ; but soon that glow
Of shame she checks, and, tranquil now,
Raising her soft-fringed eyelids dim,
Bends full her starry gaze on him.

O what a heaven, what land unknown
To Julian's happy sight is shown !
To all his agonies, all his sighs
What opening, sudden paradise !
Abandoned to that glorious gaze,
A moment in sweet dread he stays :
That gaze of speechless amethyst,
Its meaning, could it e'er be missed ?
He takes her hand inflamed with bliss,
Her willing, trembling hand in his ;
And in glad tears she hides her face
Lock'd in his passionate embrace.

To his her darling cheek is prest,
Against her own his fever'd breast ;
Love gleams from her eyes into his
In answer to each glowing kiss.
And while a smile, a sigh there springs,
Kisses and tears,—sweet idle things,

Things dearer than the world is worth,
In speech their brimming hearts break forth
Words that with ravishing music pierce
Each other's hearts, each other's ears.
Hers are dim murmurs, his a voice
That makes the silent air rejoice.

Health glows upon their cheeks, its flood
Courses impetuous in their blood ;
They feel like some absorbing truth
The fulness of their godlike youth,
Its strength, its beauty, its delight
O'erflows their bosoms, fills their sight.
And all this garden, all this glade,
Water and wind and flower and shade,
The leaves that sigh, the bird that sings
Seem one ambrosial chain of things,
One happy whole, where they are parts.
It is the fragrance of their hearts
That the rose breathes : the water's sound
Answers a feeling near, profound,
And flashing, eddying fast and bright
It leaps with their own heart's delight.
Those spheres of solemn light on high
Shine but in glorious sympathy,
And heaven seems for no other end
Spread there, but over them to bend.
Theirs is the pomp, theirs is the power
Of Nature in this sovereign hour.
For them the balmy woodlands show
Their virgin wealth : the hyacinths grow
For them, for them the nightingale
Tells all her rich melodious tale.
Earth seems one flowery empire green
And they its happy king and queen.

Elegy.

Where breathes who bloomless left the meadows !
She !
Grave, in the wintriness of thee ?
Her laughter might have thrilled the dead,
So real she seemed, so white and red :
Gone, and the aching world she widows
With me !

O, of her presence any rumour,
Spring,
News of her sweetness canst thou bring ?
In that mysterious underground
What charm, what fire, what fragrance bound ?
There, from whence bursts the whole bright summer
On wing !

Her glorious kinsfolk, that forsook us,
Wake :
Each lily, for the light's own sake.
But she, more strong, more swift to bloom,
Kept captive in the cold earth's gloom,
Will she not with the beaming crocus
Upbreak ?

Too well thy heart, bereaved lover,
Knows,
'Tis dust that did her bloom compose :
And she, so vivid and so sweet,
Is now a name, an image fleet ;
All that the stars remember of her,
A rose !